Follow the Money

Follow the Money

Smart Start: A Guide for Maximizing Your Retirement Plan

Rodney T. McNeil

Rodney T. McNeil
Follow the Money
Smart Start: A Guide for Maximizing Your Retirement Plan

Published by Spines
ISBN: 979-8-90222-739-7

Spines

TABLE OF CONTENTS

Acknowledgments xi

About the Author xv

Foreword By Ramona S. xxi

Introduction xxvii

PART ONE: 1
THE FOUNDATION

Laying the Groundwork: Why Your 401(k) Is the First Step to Financial Freedom 1

The Misconceptions About 401(k) Plans 2

The Missing Education in Employee Benefits 3

The Key to Retirement Planning: Just Start 3

Start Small, but Start Now 4

The Power of Gradual Increases 4

How Small Contributions Grow Over Time 5

Compounding Interest: The Silent Wealth Builder 6

Employer Contributions: Free Money You Can't Afford to Miss 6

The Power of Employer Matching Contributions 7

How to Take the First Step 8

Your Financial Future Is in Your Hands 9

PART TWO: 10
TAKING ACTION

Enrolling, Contributing, and Building Momentum: Getting Started with Your 401(k) 10

Understanding the Tools and Resources 11

Getting Started: A Step-by-Step Approach 11

Monitoring Your Investments 12

Why a 401(k) Is the First Step—Not the Only Step 13

What Happens When You Leave Your Employer? 13
The Long-Term Commitment to Financial Success 14

PART THREE: 15
MASTERING THE TOOLS
Navigating the Dashboard: Understanding Your 401(k) Portal and Resources 15
Navigating the 401(k) Dashboard 15
Maximizing Employer-Sponsored Resources 16
Developing Your Investment Strategy 17
Avoiding Common Pitfalls 19
Taking the First Step 19

PART FOUR: 20
MY JOURNEY BEGINS
From Novice to Advocate: How I Took My First Step and Started Teaching Others 20
The Power of Guidance and Diversification 21
Expanding My Contributions and Learning More 21
Encouraging Others to Take the First Step 22
Taking Financial Education Into My Own Hands 22
Recognizing My Purpose 23
(My Experience 2) 25
Helping Others Set and Achieve Their Goals 25
Encouraging Ownership and Long-Term Planning 26
Navigating Economic Shifts and Market Trends 26
Experience with Various Retirement Plans 27
A Personalized Approach to Financial Education 28
Personal Testimonies and a Passion for Helping Others 28
Why I Decided to Share My Experience 29
The Role of Financial Advisors 29
A Message to Everyone With a 401(k) 30

PART FIVE: 31
LEARNING THROUGH CRISIS

Staying the Course: Lessons from the 2008 Crash and Market Volatility 31
Lessons from the 2008 Market Crash 31
Staying Committed to the Plan 32
The Market Moves Two Ways – Be Prepared 33

PART SIX: 34
EMPOWERING FAMILY

Helping My Sister Retire: Real-Life Lessons in Rebuilding and Recovery 34
Helping My Sister Build a Retirement Plan 34
The Reality Check: Overcoming Debt and Low Contributions 35
Building a New Plan for Success 36
Helping Others Achieve Financial Freedom 38
The Power of a Well-Planned Retirement 39
My Purpose: Serving Others 40

PART SEVEN: 41
HABITS FOR SUCCESS

Consistency Over Time: Building Strong Habits for Lifelong Retirement Success 41
Building Strong Financial Habits for Retirement 41
The Power of Employer Matching Contributions 42
The 90-Day Rule: Regular Plan Reviews 43
Employer Contributions Vary – But Your Commitment Shouldn't 45
Retirement Is Your Responsibility—No One Else's 46

PART EIGHT: 47
STRATEGIC GROWTH

My Path to a Strong 401(k): Step-by-Step Growth Through Discipline and Planning 47
My Personal Journey to Building a Strong 401(k) Balance 47
Laying the Foundation: My First Year in a 401(k) Plan 48

A Strategic Approach: How I Increased My Contributions 48
Why Increasing Contributions Matters 49
Rolling Over My 401(k) to an IRA with Fidelity 50
The Importance of Starting Now 51
Your Financial Future Is in Your Hands 52
Final Thoughts: The Power of Taking the First Step 52

PART NINE: *MARKET MASTERY* 54
Weathering the Storm: Recovering from Market Downturns with Data-Driven Decisions 54
Lessons Learned Through Market Volatility 54
Navigating Market Corrections: Lessons from the 2022 Downturn 55
Client Success Stories and Recovery Outcomes 58
Embracing the Calling to Serve 60

PART TEN: *EXPANDING THE VISION* 62
Beyond the 401(k): Exploring Other Tools for Retirement Security 62
Setting the Vision for Retirement 62
Exploring Life After the 401(k) 63
Seeking Professional Guidance 64
The Road to Financial Freedom 66

PART ELEVEN: *LESSONS IN TRUST* 68
A Painful Mistake: Losing Half My 401(k) and Learning to Take Control 68
Your 401(k) Is Just a Click Away – Expanded 68
A Costly Lesson in Trust and Oversight – Expanded 69
Taking Ownership of My Financial Future – Expanded 70
Your Responsibility, Your Future – Expanded 71

PART TWELVE: 73
FULL CIRCLE
Understanding the 401(k): The Final Step in Building a Secure Future 73
Understanding the Foundation: What Is a 401(k) Plan? 73
Vesting, Portability, and Withdrawal Options 74
Why This Knowledge Matters 75
A Final Word of Thanks 76

PART THIRTEEN: 77
THE TRANSITION AND THE CONCLUSION
Life After the 401(k): Transitioning, Reflecting, and Owning Your Financial Future 77
Planning for the Next Chapter: What Comes After Separation 77
What Happens If You Leave Your Funds with Your Former Employer 78
Why the Lump-Sum Option Often Costs You More Than You Think 79
The Rollover IRA: A Smart, Strategic Move 80
Introducing the "Four Legs of the Stool" Retirement Strategy 81
Avoiding Common Retirement Pitfalls 82
Stay In Control: Be the Captain of Your Financial Vessel 83
The Final Step: Reflect, Refocus, Reclaim 83

PART FOURTEEN: 85
THE FIRST STEP – PATIENCE AND PASSION
How to Save with a 401(k) Investing Plan 85
Why Early Participation Matters 86
Understanding Investment Options 88
Why These Sectors Matter to Your 401(k) 92
How to Rebalance and Reallocate Your Investments 92
Developing Financial Awareness and Market Insight 94
Teaching Others Through Personal Experience 95

Patience and Passion: The Two Pillars of Success 96
Final Thoughts 96

PART FIFTEEN: 98
MY REVELATIONS: PURPOSE, PATIENCE, AND PERSONAL GROWTH
A Journey Beyond Numbers 98
The Measure of True Wealth 98
Humility in Teaching and Learning 99
A Simple Truth About the Market 100
The Power of Staying Committed 100
The Foundation of Financial Literacy 101
RM Chart LLC: My Platform to Serve 102
A Call to Action: Your Future Is in Your Hands 103
Final Reflections 104

Acknowledgments

I would like to thank my wife, Tessa, for her unwavering love, strength, and support during our lifetime together. She has given me the space to work and create this manuscript and build my company as a testimony of my growth and evolution in business while serving others. I also want to thank my son R.J., whose will and determination encourage me to move forward. I love you both, my family.

Special thanks to my mother and father, the late Eunice and Aaron Wilcox, whose life of love, sacrifice, and perseverance gave me the foundation needed while raising my siblings and me during tough times growing up in Miami, Florida. She was a shining example of overcoming adversity. She taught me the value of money and helped me with my first job working at a fruit stand with a local vendor. That was both a challenge and a reward at the young age of 7. Thank you, Momma, for being my rock and confidant. And I miss you every day.

I want to thank my sisters, Lorraine and Tawanna, and my brothers, Mikel, Jerry, and Brice, for being the examples and inspirations to bring out the best in me. Our growing up together was a journey of exploration, discovery, fellowship, blood, sweat, and tears. I am battle-tested because of each of you. And I love you all.

I also want to thank my Uncle, Aaron McNeil, and his family, for their love and support. Thank you, Uncle Aaron, for mentoring me during my formidable years. And thank you to my biological father, the late Ernest McNeil, for our mended relationship and healing prior to his passing.

I want to recognize and thank the men whose influences over the years were paramount to my development. Thank you, Dale T., Kelvin M., Darryl F., Richard F., Chad H., and the late Coach Jacob Caldwell of Miami Jackson High School.

I also want to thank all my Family members in Miami, Florida; Beaufort, South Carolina or “The Hill”; Savannah, Georgia; and Lafayette, Louisiana, who are my roots of influence, education, and strength.

Special thanks and recognition to “The Edgebrook Team” in Houston, Texas, which gave me the catalyst to write this book. We all started with a “PIE” Chart! Thank you, Lina, Martha, Maggie, Jose R., Sonia, Omaira, Valery, Rosa, Ruby, Mari, Rosemary, and Jessie.

Special mention and thanks to my classmates of The Miami Jackson Senior High Class of 1983 for our faith, strength, and friendship. I am a General for life!

And finally, thank you, Brett and Adam, of TTG Mastermind, for the opportunity to be a part of your business and trading community. Finally, thank you to all of my clients, friends, and associates whom I have served over the years. Thank you all for giving me the inspiration to write this book.

About the Author

Rodney McNeil is an entrepreneur, consultant, and financial literacy advocate. He is a native of Miami, Florida, where he attended Miami Jackson Senior High School. Upon graduation, he accepted a scholarship from the University of Louisiana at Lafayette, where he earned a Bachelor of Science degree in Industrial Technology & Engineering. Throughout his career, he has worked in the fields of banking and finance, engineering, and personnel management. His education and experience have afforded him the ability to start his own business. He currently resides in the Houston, Texas, metropolitan area.

Customer Testimonials for "Follow the Money"

"Rodney, I can truly say that investing with you over these past few years has been more of an adventure for me. It's like uncharted waters and unforeseen shorelines—always something new, better, and different on the horizon. Each time we talk, I see and feel a calm excitement in your voice, letting me know that investing is about patience, endurance, and that no financial opportunity is without risk. I look forward to the next chapter."

— Dwayne R.
Melville, Louisiana

"Before working with Rodney, I had very limited knowledge about investing or how the market worked. I simply knew I wanted to retire with confidence and security. Rodney took the time to explain everything clearly, without overwhelming me, and always with a calm and encouraging approach that made me feel at ease.

Since becoming his client, I've seen significant growth in my portfolio—more than I ever expected. I now feel informed, empowered, and far more prepared for retirement.

I truly appreciate the care and dedication Rodney brings to his work. His guidance has not only improved my financial outlook but has given me real peace of mind."

— **Marsha N.**
Oklahoma City, Oklahoma

"I don't quite know how to put into words the knowledge Rodney has shared and the lessons he has taught me on how to take care of my money by placing my retirement first and not putting it off until later! Your ability to explain in terms I can understand and take action is vital for my success. Thank you!"

— **Erana R.**
Melville, Louisiana

"About four years ago, my business partner shared with me that his cousin was managing his 401(k). He would consistently say to me, 'You need to get with Mr. Rodney.'

After working on my job for over 20 years, I was embarrassed about my lack of knowledge and the amount I had accumulated. Hesitantly, I scheduled a Zoom call. Rodney was professional, respectful, knowledgeable, and down-to-earth. I left our first meeting so excited that I couldn't sleep.

Three years later, not only am I excited—I have a phenomenal strategic plan, and my 401(k) has tripled since the first year. Investing about 24 hours a year has changed my life. That's why I now tell everyone: 'You need to get with Mr. Rodney!!'"

— Vernon A.
Ridgeway, South Carolina

"I've known Rodney for over 40 years. In the last year and a half, I've learned a lot about stocks, bonds, CDs, 401(k)s, and how to diversify my portfolio. He's patient, listens to your concerns, and explains things as many times as needed.

Since my conversations with Rodney, I've made money and now understand my finances and retirement. He always says, 'Follow the money'—and now I do."

— David P.
Miami, Florida

"Before I started working with Rodney McNeil a year and a half ago, I felt overwhelmed and unsure about my financial future. I had a 401(k), but I wasn't confident in its growth. From our first meeting, Rodney took the time to understand my needs and put together a strategy tailored to my goals.

Thanks to his guidance, my 401(k) has doubled in value, and my Roth IRA is also seeing growth. I never imagined this was possible in such a short time.

Rodney's financial expertise is matched by his character—patient, trustworthy, and encouraging. We share joy in my financial progress and laugh over the nickname he gave me: 'Holiday Rally.' I highly recommend him to anyone looking to secure their future."

— **Cassandra J.**
Columbia, South Carolina

"When I first met Rodney, I was overwhelmed by all the facts about 401(k)s. My friend Dolores told me he could help. My 401(k) had just been sitting there.

I'm so grateful I met a trustworthy financial advisor. Now, together, we are following the money. I thank God for putting Rodney in my life to guide me through this journey."

— **Esther P.**
Pearland, Texas

"I truly thank my Father God for allowing me the opportunity to be introduced to Rodney. I can't thank him enough for the incredible impact he's had on my financial literacy—especially with my 401(k) and stock market investments.

Rodney took time to understand my goals and gave me personalized advice. I've learned the importance of diversifying, reallocating assets, and continually investing in myself.

His patience and support have given me the confidence to take control of my money. I couldn't be more grateful."

— Thomas F.
Nashville, Tennessee

Foreword By Ramona S.

Client Perspective on Personalized Financial Guidance

Navigating the complex world of personal finance can be a daunting task, especially in an era marked by volatility and uncertainty. However, the financial services we receive from RM Chart, LLC, and Mr. McNeil have truly been a beacon of clarity and reassurance. This testimonial aims to convey the profound impact that professional and trusting financial guidance has had on our lives, transforming not just our monetary situation but also our overall sense of security, confidence, and peace of mind.

Initial Challenges and the Search for Expertise

Before being introduced to Mr. McNeil at RM Chart, LLC, I was overwhelmed by the myriad of options and decisions that modern financial planning entails, and my attempt to navigate the complex world of investing independently was daunting. From planning for retirement to understanding who to trust, how, what, and when to invest, my knowledge was fragmented, and my confidence wavered. I relied on bank financial advisors and other financial entities to make financial investment decisions for me. I remained uninformed, dependent, and financial gain was minimal. I remained challenged in search for financial guidance that I could understand, rely on, and trust. Recognizing the need, I decided to partner with Mr. Rodney McNeil of RM Chart, LLC. It was one of the best decisions I have ever made for my family and me.

A Tailored Financial Roadmap

The first meeting and those that follow are nothing short of enlightening. During the initial consultation, Mr. McNeil took the time to understand our unique financial circumstances, concerns, and aspirations. Instead of offering generic advice, he educated us and focused on crafting a tailored financial roadmap that aligned with my family's personal and financial goals. What stood out immediately was his genuine interest in what was important to us, taking the time and ability to simplify complex financial concepts and making it easy to understand how each decision—whether it pertains to budgeting, saving, or investing—will impact our overall financial health and future. This clarity gave us the knowledge and confidence to take ownership of our financial future.

A Relationship Built on Trust

What truly sets Mr. McNeil and the services he provides apart from others is the personalized relationships he fosters with his clients. He exemplifies a holistic and faith-based approach to the guidance provided to clients and demonstrates an unwavering God-centered dedication, integrity, and professionalism. Mr. McNeil consistently goes above and beyond, ensuring we remain informed and satisfied, whether by addressing questions or providing timely updates and recommending portfolio changes during market fluctuations. We never feel like just another client. The personalized attention and genuine concern for me and my family's financial future and well-being make all the difference. He has earned our trust through transparency, reliability, and a commitment to excellence.

Looking Ahead

As I continue my financial journey, I am finally confident that I have the tools, knowledge, and trusted support to navigate this complex world of personal finance and plan for my family's financial future. This partnership has not only improved my financial outlook but has also enhanced our quality of life. For anyone considering professional financial services, I wholeheartedly recommend taking the leap. Sound guidance, from a trusting and competent financial advisor, can open doors to opportunities you never thought possible, and the sense of empowerment it brings is truly invaluable.

Results That Speak Volumes

Since implementing the strategies recommended by Mr. McNeil, the results have been remarkable. Our savings have grown steadily, and we now feel confident about the trajectory of our investments. More importantly, we have a clear vision of how to achieve our short and long-term goals.

Wealth Growth Through Smart Investments

Mr. McNeil's expertise in financial planning and investment strategies has been particularly impactful. He identifies diversified opportunities tailored to our financial objectives, balancing growth with stability. Regular meetings, reviews, and adjustments to our portfolios ensure that they remain aligned with market changes and our evolving needs.

Peace of Mind

The greatest testament to RM Chart, LLC service is the peace of mind we now enjoy. Knowing that our finances are in capable hands allows us to focus on other aspects of our lives, free from stress and the uncertainty that once plagued us. This newfound confidence extends to my family as well, as we now have a secure plan for the future.

Conclusion

In a world where financial security often feels elusive, the services I receive from RM Chart and Mr. McNeil are nothing short of transformative. He is a teacher and disciple of God, sharing his gift with others, committed to educating and helping people navigate the complexities of investing. This testimonial is a heartfelt expression of gratitude for the professionalism, expertise, and care that have made all the difference. Our journey is a testament to the power of informed, strategic financial planning, and we are excited to see what the future holds. To anyone seeking peace of mind, sound financial guidance, and security, my advice is simple: Invest in a professional financial advisor that you can trust, rely on, and who can provide the needed support along the journey. It is an investment in yourself, family, goals, and dreams.

Introduction

This book is the beginning or starting point for anyone who wants to gain a better understanding of how to START building a financial plan for their future. Over the past 20 years, I have learned and discovered how to create a roadmap for myself to peek into my future and achieve my financial goals. It was a combination of my personal evolution, interviews, interactive experiences, consistent self-study, and education that afforded me the skills and determination to learn how to build my confidence and understanding of financial literacy and market terminology. Eventually, I was able to share what I learned with others.

I believe the key to understanding your retirement goals is to set your financial targets and start to "Pay Yourself First!"

This can and will be an ongoing process once you begin. For myself, it was a personal journey and fantastic voyage as I encountered several turbulent time periods, choppy waters, and eventually smooth sailing when I discovered my own financial identity. I believe you can do it too! No matter your age, you have to just START! Welcome aboard!

PART ONE:
THE FOUNDATION

Laying the Groundwork: Why Your 401(k) Is the First Step to Financial Freedom

Many people don't fully understand how to utilize and maximize their 401(k) plan through their employer. Some financial voices even claim that a 401(k) isn't the best way to invest for the future.

I strongly disagree. The 401(k) was introduced in the mid-1970s as a replacement for pension plans, and while it did shift the responsibility of retirement savings from employers to employees, we cannot afford to ignore this opportunity today.

It was actually my sister, Miss Supervisor, who first opened my eyes to how often people overlook their 401(k) benefits. I reminded her, "You might not understand your benefits, but you must learn how to maximize your plan."

A 401(k) may not be perfect, but it offers working-class individuals a structured way to save for retirement. More importantly, many employers provide matching contributions ranging from 3% to 6%, essentially giving you free money to grow your savings. While a 401(k) alone may not guarantee a comfortable retirement, it provides a critical foundation—if you know how to use it wisely.

The Misconceptions About 401(k) Plans

Many employees assume that contributing 5% of their salary, especially when matched dollar-for-dollar by their employer, will be enough for retirement. While this is a solid start, it's not enough to build substantial wealth over time.

With the right strategy, you can position yourself for a much stronger financial future. Your 401(k) can serve as a stepping stone to a rollover IRA or a managed investment plan when you change employers or retire. However, most people don't receive the guidance they need to make informed decisions about their retirement savings.

One major misconception is that 401(k) plans have limited investment options. While the investment choices may not be as broad as those found in an IRA, most 401(k) plans offer a range of mutual funds, target-date funds, and index funds that allow you to diversify your portfolio. By selecting the right mix of investments based on your risk tolerance and time horizon, you can maximize your potential growth.

Another myth is that 401(k) plans are expensive due to administrative fees. It's true that some plans have fees, but many employers negotiate lower-cost investment options for their employees. Additionally, the tax advantages of a 401(k) often outweigh any associated fees, making it a worthwhile investment vehicle for long-term growth.

The Missing Education in Employee Benefits

When you start a new job, your HR department provides a benefits package that includes health insurance, dental coverage, and often a 401(k) or 403(b) plan. However, what employers don't do is educate their employees on how to maximize these benefits.

I learned this firsthand over 20 years ago while working in the financial industry. I made it my mission to understand how these plans worked and how to make the most of them. Unfortunately, most employees are left to figure it out on their own, without any clear guidance or educational resources.

Even worse, many employees mistakenly believe that enrolling in the plan and setting up contributions is enough. But a passive approach to a 401(k) can limit its potential. Employees need to actively manage their investments, reassess their contributions regularly, and take advantage of any employer-provided financial literacy resources.

To ensure that you're getting the most out of your 401(k), take the time to review your investment choices, rebalance your portfolio periodically, and increase your contributions as your salary grows. Many employers also offer financial planning seminars or online tools—take advantage of these resources to improve your understanding of retirement planning.

The Key to Retirement Planning: Just Start

One of the biggest misconceptions about saving for retirement is that you need to start with a large amount of money. This couldn't be further from the truth. The most important thing isn't how much you contribute at first—it's that you start. Even small, consistent contributions can grow into a significant retirement fund over time thanks to the power of compounding interest and employer matching contributions.

Start Small, but Start Now

Many people hesitate to enroll in their employer-sponsored retirement plan because they feel they can't afford to contribute much. But the beauty of a 401(k) or 403(b) plan is that you don't have to start big. If you contribute just 1% of your salary and your employer matches it dollar for dollar, you are immediately doubling your savings.

For example, if you earn $50,000 per year, 1% of your salary is $500. If your employer matches that amount, your

total contributions for the year become $1,000. That may not seem like a lot at first, but over time, as these contributions continue and earn interest, that number grows exponentially.

Even if 1% is all you can afford right now, starting with that small percentage gets you into the habit of saving. Once you're comfortable, you can increase your contributions incrementally —by just 1% or 2% each year—without drastically impacting your take-home pay.

The Power of Gradual Increases

The best strategy for long-term growth is to gradually increase your contributions over time. By committing to raising your contributions by just 2% per year, you can steadily build your retirement savings without feeling a major financial burden.

Let's look at how this strategy works:

- **Year 1:** You contribute 3% of your salary. If your employer matches 3%, your total annual contribution is 6%.
- **Year 2:** You increase your contribution to 5%. With a 3% employer match, you're now at 8%.
- **Year 3:** You bump it up to 7%, bringing your total savings rate (including employer match) to 10%.
- **Year 5:** You're contributing 10%, and with the employer match, your total savings rate is now 13%.

This gradual approach ensures that your savings grow steadily without creating financial strain. Before you know it, you'll be contributing 10% to 15% of your income—putting you on track to accumulate six figures in your retirement account within a decade.

How Small Contributions Grow Over Time

To truly understand the impact of saving early and consistently, let's consider a real-world example. Suppose you contribute just $100 per month to your 401(k), and your employer matches that amount for a total of $200 monthly savings. Assuming an average annual return of 7%, here's how your savings could grow:

- **After 5 years:** $14,300
- **After 10 years:** $34,400
- **After 20 years:** $102,000
- **After 30 years:** $240,000

And this is with just $100 per month! If you contribute more over time, your retirement savings will increase even faster.

Compounding Interest: The Silent Wealth Builder

What makes this strategy so powerful is compounding interest—the process of earning interest on both your initial contributions and the returns they generate. The earlier you start, the more time your money has to grow.

For example, if you begin saving at 25 and invest $5,000 per year with an average return of 7%, by the time you reach 65, you'll have over **$1 million**. But if you wait until 35 to start, your total will be around **$500,000**—half as much.

This illustrates why *starting* is far more important than waiting until you can contribute a large amount.

Employer Contributions: Free Money You Can't Afford to Miss

One of the greatest benefits of a 401(k) or 403(b) plan is the employer match. Many companies offer a matching contribution of 3% to 6% of your salary. This is essentially free money that boosts your savings.

Let's say you make $60,000 per year, and your employer matches 5%. If you contribute 5% of your salary ($3,000 annually), your employer also adds $3,000, bringing your total contributions to **$6,000 per year**. Over 20 years, assuming a 7% annual return, your balance could exceed **$250,000**.

If your employer offers a match, *take full advantage of it*. Contribute at least enough to receive the full match; otherwise, you're leaving free money on the table.

The Power of Employer Matching Contributions

Let's say your employer matches up to 5% of your salary. If you contribute 5%, your employer will match it, effectively doubling your savings. This "free money" grows over time through compounding, giving you a significant financial advantage.

With steady contributions and smart investment choices, you could have anywhere from $80,000 to $100,000 saved in just 5 to 10 years. The key is consistency and discipline.

To understand the power of employer matching, consider this example: If you earn $50,000 per year and contribute 5% ($2,500), your employer will also contribute $2,500, bringing your total savings for the year to $5,000. Over 10 years, assuming an average annual return of 7%, your balance could grow to more than $80,000—without having to contribute anything extra beyond the first 5%.

Additionally, taking advantage of tax-deferred growth in a traditional 401(k) or tax-free withdrawals in a Roth 401(k) can further enhance your retirement savings. Understanding these tax benefits can help you decide which type of account best fits your financial strategy.

How to Take the First Step

To start leveraging your 401(k) effectively, follow these steps:

1. **Learn About Your Employer's Plan** – Review your benefits package and understand the specific details of your company's 401(k) or 403(b) plan.
2. **Ask Questions** – Speak with your HR representative or benefits administrator to understand eligibility, employer match percentages, and vesting periods.
3. **Start Small and Increase Over Time** – If you can only afford to contribute 3% now, begin there and aim to increase your contributions by 2% annually.
4. **Diversify Your Investments** – Many 401(k) plans offer a range of investment options. Choose a mix that aligns with your long-term financial goals.
5. **Commit to the Process** – Saving for retirement isn't an overnight success; it's a journey that requires consistency and patience.
6. **Automate Your Contributions** – Set up automatic paycheck deductions to ensure you consistently contribute without having to think about it.
7. **Monitor and Adjust** –Review your investments periodically and adjust them based on market conditions, life changes, or retirement goals.

Your Financial Future Is in Your Hands

The reality is that no one is going to save for your retirement except you. Our country faces a growing national deficit, and inflation continues to make saving more difficult. That's why it's critical to take control of your financial future now.

Even if you start by contributing just $10 per paycheck, you're making progress. The most important thing is to start. Your future self will thank you for the decisions you make today.

By taking the first step and committing to a long-term savings strategy, you are setting yourself up for financial security and peace of mind in retirement. It's never too late—or too early—to begin.

Let's take the first step together.

PART TWO:
TAKING ACTION

Enrolling, Contributing, and Building Momentum: Getting Started with Your 401(k)

Once you've spoken with your employer's Human Resources or Benefits Director and enrolled in the company-sponsored 401(k) plan, you're ready to take the next step.

The first thing you should do is ask your Benefits Director about two key details:

1. What is the company's maximum matching contribution?
2. How much are you allowed to contribute?

This information will help you determine your initial contribution, which typically starts at 1% to 3% of your salary. The sooner you begin, the more time your money has to grow. Once you've set your contribution, it will automatically be deducted from your paycheck in the next payroll cycle.

Understanding the Tools and Resources

To maximize the benefits of your 401(k), it's essential to learn how to use the tools and resources available within your employer's plan. However, many employees find financial and market terminology overwhelming, which makes it difficult to navigate their investment options effectively.

With over 20 years of experience in the financial sector, I have dedicated my career to educating individuals on how to maximize their 401(k) and 403(b) plans. Through one-on-one consultations, I guide clients throughout the year, helping them take full control of their financial future. My background in banking and financial services has allowed me to support clients in employer-sponsored, self-directed 401(k) plans with measurable success.

Getting Started: A Step-by-Step Approach

When I work with clients, we always start with the basics:

1. **Gain Access** – Create a username and password to log in to your plan's online portal.
2. **Request a Self-Directed Plan** – Ask your benefits administrator if you can opt for a self-directed 401(k) rather than a managed plan. A self-directed plan gives you more control over your investment choices.
3. **Determine Your Matching Contribution** – Start with at least 1% to 5% to take full advantage of employer contributions.

4. **Learn the System** – Get familiar with your employer's plan tools and resources to track and manage your investments.
5. **Set a Goal and Build a Plan** – Define your long-term financial goals and create an investment strategy to achieve them.

Diversification is a crucial aspect of a successful retirement plan. Most employer-sponsored plans offer a selection of funds or investments to choose from. By spreading your contributions across different investment types, you can reduce risk and increase potential returns.

Monitoring Your Investments

After selecting your investments, I recommend waiting at least 30 days before reviewing your contributions and balance. This allows your portfolio to adjust to market conditions and gives you a clearer picture of how well your selections align with your financial goals.

In my business, I provide **free one-on-one consultations via Zoom** to educate my clients and build long-term relationships with them. I encourage each client to commit to monthly meetings for at least a year. These sessions focus on:

- Understanding financial markets and their impact on retirement savings.
    - The role of the Federal Reserve, inflation, and economic trends.

- Navigating employer-provided investment tools and strategies.

This learning process is **educational, enlightening, and empowering**. Financial literacy gives you the confidence you need to take control of your investments and plan for your future.

Why a 401(k) Is the First Step—Not the Only Step

A 401(k) is not a guaranteed retirement solution, but it is an essential first step. Anyone working in corporate America or for an employer offering this benefit should take full advantage of it. Employer-matching contributions are essentially **free money**, and failing to contribute means leaving money on the table.

Unfortunately, many individuals are unaware of their ability to start saving while they are employed. In our society, a large percentage of people do not even have enough savings for an emergency, let alone retirement. The key to financial security is simple: **Ask questions and start now**. Whether you're in your 20s or your 50s, it's never too late to take action.

What Happens When You Leave Your Employer?

If you have a 401(k) in place and leave your employer, you still have options. You don't have to leave your money behind. In fact, I strongly recommend rolling over your 401(k) into another qualified plan, such as an IRA, to avoid unnecessary tax penalties and maintain investment growth.

During my monthly consultations, I help clients navigate these transitions, ensuring they make informed decisions about their retirement funds. Learning about investment strategies and financial planning is an ongoing journey, and staying informed will help you maximize your savings potential.

The Long-Term Commitment to Financial Success

Many employees contribute only the bare minimum—typically 1% to 3%—to their retirement plans and see minimal growth. Others are unaware of how to build their savings more effectively. The truth is, with the right knowledge and consistency, you can accelerate your retirement savings and reach your financial goals faster than you might think.

Helping others build their retirement plans has been my passion for over two decades. During my time in the banking industry, I learned the fundamental principles of how money works and, more importantly, how anyone can take control of their financial future with the right education and discipline. **Patience and commitment are the keys to success.**

Looking back, I realize that my career in finance was no accident. I was placed here for a reason—to serve others. By guiding people on their journey to financial independence, I fulfill my purpose. The journey to retirement planning starts with one simple step: **Just start**.

PART THREE:
MASTERING THE TOOLS

Navigating the Dashboard: Understanding Your 401(k) Portal and Resources

Now that you have successfully gained access to your employer's retirement plan online, it's time to explore the **dashboard and key resources** that will help you understand and manage your 401(k) effectively. This is the foundation of **taking control of your financial future** and ensuring that you maximize the benefits of your employer-sponsored retirement plan.

Navigating the 401(k) Dashboard

A well-structured retirement plan platform provides various **tools and resources** to guide you through the process of self-directing your investments. Understanding how to use these features will give you the confidence to take control of your financial future.

As you navigate the site, you may see tabs such as:

- **Manage My Account** – Your central hub for making adjustments and tracking performance.

- **View My Investments** – Displays your current holdings and asset allocation.
- **Account Summary** – Provides an overview of your total balance and contributions.
- **Balance Details** – Tracks your financial growth over time and highlights trends in your savings.
- **Return on Investment (ROI)** – Shows how much your investments have earned compared to your contributions.
- **Fund Performance** – Displays year-to-date (YTD) returns on selected funds and their historical trends.
- **Manage My Contributions** – Allows you to adjust contribution levels based on plan limits and employer match opportunities.
- **Research and Tools** – Includes calculators, charts, and educational resources to help you make informed decisions about your portfolio.

Each of these tools plays a vital role in **understanding how your 401(k) functions** and how to **manage it effectively for long-term success**. Familiarizing yourself with these features will allow you to confidently navigate your retirement plan.

Maximizing Employer-Sponsored Resources

One of the biggest advantages of a 401(k) is the **support system provided by your employer**. Most companies offer educational resources, financial planning tools, and even **consultations with**

benefits administrators or financial advisors to help employees understand their options.

Your **benefits administrator** is a valuable resource when starting or managing your 401(k) plan. If you ever have questions about the dashboard, contribution limits, investment options, or **how to maximize your benefits**, don't hesitate to reach out for guidance. Many administrators can walk you through the online platform and explain how to **utilize its tools effectively**.

If your company offers **financial wellness seminars or one-on-one retirement planning sessions**, take full advantage of them. These resources can provide deeper insights into topics like:

- The impact of **compound interest** on your long-term savings
- Strategies for **diversifying** your portfolio to manage risk
- Understanding the **tax advantages** of pre-tax and Roth contributions
- Planning for different life stages, from early career to pre-retirement

Developing Your Investment Strategy

Once I learned how to navigate my employer's retirement plan platform, I was able to gradually **create and refine my investment strategy** based on my long-term financial goals. This process takes time, and there is no rush—**learning is ongoing**.

What matters most is that you **start engaging with the resources available** and take an active role in your financial future.

To develop a successful investment strategy, consider these key steps:

1. **Understand Your Risk Tolerance** – Are you comfortable with high-risk, high-reward investments, or do you prefer stability?
2. **Diversify Your Portfolio** – A balanced mix of stocks, bonds, and target-date funds can help reduce risk.
3. **Review Fund Performance** – Regularly check your fund's returns and historical performance to ensure they align with your goals.
4. **Rebalance Your Investments** – Over time, market fluctuations may shift your portfolio allocation. Adjust periodically to maintain your intended balance.
5. **Increase Contributions Over Time** – As your salary grows, increase your contributions to maximize employer matching and compound interest benefits.

Every tool, chart, and performance metric serves a purpose. The more comfortable you become with these features, the more **confident and strategic** you will be in managing your retirement savings.

Avoiding Common Pitfalls

Many employees fail to take full advantage of their 401(k) plans due to common mistakes such as the following:

- **Not contributing enough to get the full employer match** – This is essentially leaving free money on the table.
- **Ignoring investment options** – Defaulting to a single fund without evaluating performance and risk can limit growth.
- **Failing to rebalance their portfolio** – Without adjustments, your investments may become too risky or too conservative over time.
- **Withdrawing early** – Cashing out before retirement can result in **penalties and loss of future earnings**.

By actively managing your 401(k) and taking advantage of the available tools, you can avoid these pitfalls and set yourself up for financial success.

Taking the First Step

Retirement planning is a **journey, not a destination**. By utilizing the tools and resources available to you, asking questions, and continuously learning, you will set yourself up for long-term success. The sooner you take control of your retirement savings, the greater the rewards will be.

Take the first step today—**your future self will thank you.**

PART FOUR:
MY JOURNEY BEGINS

From Novice to Advocate: How I Took My First Step and Started Teaching Others

Twenty years ago, while working as a manager in the banking industry, I took my first step toward securing my financial future—I enrolled in my employer's 401(k) plan.

I started by speaking with the benefits administrator at my company to understand the plan's contribution requirements and employer matching policy. At the time, my employer offered a 5% match. Wanting to ease into the process, I began with a **1% contribution for the first 30 days** to familiarize myself with how the plan worked.

The following month, I increased my contribution to **3%**, allowing me to observe how my savings grew over time. By the **third month**, I raised my contribution to **5%** and maintained it for the remainder of my first year. Watching my balance grow gave me confidence, and I started to grasp the importance of disciplined investing.

The Power of Guidance and Diversification

My mentor, a benefits administrator, played a crucial role in my early success. He took the time to explain how the 401(k) worked and emphasized the importance of **diversification**. I learned that spreading my investments across different funds would help manage risk and maximize long-term gains.

Additionally, I was introduced to the concept of **rebalancing and reallocating** my investments. This knowledge allowed me to make informed adjustments to my portfolio based on both short-term and long-term goals. I realized that I wasn't just saving money—I was strategically planning for my future.

By the end of my **first full year**, my 401(k) had grown to **$12,000**. My mentor congratulated me, noting that many employees never take the time to understand their retirement plans. He was right; most people overlook the tools and resources available to them, missing out on valuable growth opportunities simply due to a lack of knowledge.

Expanding My Contributions and Learning More

In my **second year**, I increased my contributions to **7%**, while my employer continued to match up to **5%**. I also took a proactive approach, logging into my 401(k) portal regularly to explore its tools and resources. Each month, I noticed **steady growth** in my retirement savings, which reinforced my belief in the plan's effectiveness.

That year, I was transferred to another company location. It was there that I began speaking with my coworkers about their 401(k) participation, and to my surprise, **most of them were either contributing the bare minimum or not participating at all**. Additionally, many had little understanding of how the plan worked or how it could benefit them in the long run.

Encouraging Others to Take the First Step

I quickly realized a common misconception—many employees didn't recognize that their employer match was **free money**. I encouraged my coworkers to contribute at least **enough to receive the full match**, explaining that even small contributions could have a significant impact over time.

For example, if an employee earned **$100 per pay period** and the employer offered a **5% match**, the company would contribute an additional **$5** to their plan. If the employee also contributed **5%**, they would be investing **$10 per paycheck**—a simple but effective way to grow retirement savings.

While some employers offer **less than a 5% match**, the key takeaway is the same: **Start now and take advantage of what's available**. Even if you can only afford a small percentage at first, it's better than waiting and losing out on the power of compounding.

Taking Financial Education Into My Own Hands

At my new location, I decided to take action. I organized **monthly after-hours sessions** where I would guide my coworkers through the process of setting up and managing their 401(k) plans.

Each session covered the fundamentals, including:

- Logging into the 401(k) portal and navigating its features
- Understanding investment options and contribution limits
- Learning how to **rebalance and diversify** a portfolio
- Setting financial goals for retirement

The primary requirement for 401(k) participation is **vesting**—the period of time an employee must work before gaining full ownership of employer contributions. Most companies have a vesting period of **one to five years**, after which employees are entitled to keep their employer-matched funds even if they leave the company.

After just **six months**, most of my coworkers had enrolled in the plan. A year later, **they began seeing significant growth in their retirement accounts**. Watching their progress was incredibly fulfilling to me, as I have always had a passion for educating and empowering others.

Recognizing My Purpose

As my coworkers experienced success, they began sharing their newfound knowledge with other employees in different locations. Soon, I was receiving calls from people across the city, asking for guidance on how to **build and manage their own retirement plans**.

It didn't matter what their age or level of financial knowledge was—I welcomed anyone who was willing to learn. Through these experiences, I developed a deep sense of **gratitude** for the opportunity to help others.

As my reach expanded, I found myself advising employees from various departments, industries, and backgrounds. Some were young professionals just beginning their careers, while others were mid-career workers who had never prioritized retirement savings. Regardless of their starting point, each person had the same reaction when they realized the impact of their decisions: **Why didn't I start sooner?**

Looking back, I now understand that my journey in the financial industry wasn't just about building my own wealth; **it was about serving others.** I truly believe that financial education is one of the most powerful tools a person can have, and I am grateful to have been given the ability to articulate and share this knowledge.

Working in the banking industry taught me many valuable lessons about money, but the most important one is this: **Anyone can take control of their financial future with the right knowledge, discipline, and guidance.**

For those just starting out, the point is simple—**just take the first step.** The sooner you start, the more time you have to let your investments grow. No matter your age or current financial situation, there is always an opportunity to build a secure future. And if you ever feel uncertain, remember—there are people out there, like I once was, who are more than willing to help.

(My Experience 2)

Over the past two decades, my experience in the financial industry has enabled me to develop a comprehensive understanding of how individual funds and investment options within employer-sponsored plans operate. This depth of experience enables me to educate, guide, and empower individuals who wish to take a more active role in managing their finances.

Helping Others Set and Achieve Their Goals

I specialize in helping individuals establish **short-term and long-term goals** while creating a path to achieve them over time. Through my **one-on-one consultations**, I take a deep dive into the details of their retirement plans and explain the fundamentals of investing, the importance of diversification, and how different funds perform across the market.

A crucial part of my teaching process includes **reviewing charts, graphs, and historical performance data** to help individuals make informed investment decisions. I introduce them to various fund categories, such as:

- **Target-date funds** – Designed to automatically adjust asset allocation as retirement nears.
- **Growth funds** – Focused on companies with high potential for expansion.
- **Value funds** – Investing in undervalued stocks with strong fundamentals.

- **Blended funds** – A mix of growth and value stocks to balance risk and reward.
- **Bond funds** – Provide stability and income during market fluctuations.

Each of these funds falls into **large-cap, mid-cap, or small-cap classifications**, and understanding their role within a portfolio is essential to building a **well-balanced, diversified retirement strategy**.

Encouraging Ownership and Long-Term Planning

My goal is not just to teach but to **empower individuals to take ownership of their financial future**. Whether someone has a **five-year plan** or a **20-year plan**, active participation is key to building a solid retirement fund.

Once they meet their initial goals, I often recommend rolling their 401(k) into an **Individual Retirement Account (IRA)** to continue growing their wealth. Within an IRA, individuals have access to **index funds, mutual funds, and a broader range of investment opportunities** that allow for greater customization and long-term financial planning.

Navigating Economic Shifts and Market Trends

Markets are constantly evolving, and economic downturns can impact investments. That's why it's crucial to make **strategic**

adjustments based on:

- **Overall economic conditions**
- **Federal Reserve reports on inflation and interest rates**
- **Labor market trends and job growth**
- **Government policies and administrative changes**

The stock market moves in only two directions—**up and down**—, but with the right knowledge, investors can make **informed, balanced decisions** to navigate market cycles and continue growing their wealth.

Experience with Various Retirement Plans

Throughout my career, I have worked with a variety of **401(k) and 403(b) plans**, including those managed by:

- **Fidelity**
- **Vanguard**
- **Charles Schwab**
- **Nationwide**
- **TSP (Thrift Savings Plan)**
- **Florida Retirement System (FRS)**
- **Transamerica**
- **TIAA & Ready Retire**
- **Suncoast**
- **Corebridge**
- **Mass Mutual**

- **Invesco**
- **Merrill Lynch**

Although each plan has its unique offerings, the core principles remain the same—**diversification, consistency, and long-term vision are critical for success**.

A Personalized Approach to Financial Education

One of the most rewarding aspects of my work is the ability to **build personal relationships with each individual I mentor**. I often compare this journey to learning how to drive—while they are behind the wheel, I am in the passenger seat, helping them navigate the road ahead.

This process requires **patience, hands-on learning, and constant support**. In the first year, individuals gain a solid foundation. After two years, they have a strong plan in place. By the **five-year mark**, they have **a well-structured, growing retirement portfolio** that will support them for years to come.

Personal Testimonies and a Passion for Helping Others

Over the past decade, I have received numerous testimonials from individuals whom I have helped. Watching someone go from **confusion to confidence** is one of the most fulfilling aspects of my work.

A colleague once told me, **"Do what you love and love what**

you do." That statement has stayed with me, and it is reflected in my actions every day. My passion for educating and supporting people is not just a profession—it is a calling.

Why I Decided to Share My Experience

Several years ago, a family member encouraged me to **write a book** about my experiences in financial education. At the time, I brushed off the idea, believing that my work spoke for itself. But as the years passed, I realized that there are still **far too many people who lack the knowledge and resources to take control of their financial future**. That is why I am sharing this information now.

When I left the banking industry **10 years ago**, I continued helping and supporting people who sought my guidance. Then, in **the fall of 2020**, I took a leap and started my own business, dedicated to helping anyone interested in learning how to create and manage their own **self-directed 401(k) plans**.

The Role of Financial Advisors

While I focus on **educating individuals on how their 401(k) plans work**, I always encourage them to **seek professional advice** from a licensed financial advisor for long-term planning beyond their employer-sponsored retirement accounts. My goal is to ensure that every person I work with feels **confident, informed, and empowered** to take the next step.

A Message to Everyone With a 401(k)

This book is for **anyone** currently working for a company that offers a **401(k) plan**—whether they are in their **first year or their 20th year**, there is always something new to learn.

If I could go back and give my younger self one piece of advice, it would be this: **Start sooner.**

In most workplaces, employees are handed a **benefits package** and expected to figure things out on their own. There is little emphasis on the importance of starting a retirement plan early, and as a result, **many people miss out on years of financial growth**.

I am sharing this knowledge because I want to **empower every individual** I serve. Everyone deserves the opportunity to build a strong financial future—the key is to **START.**

PART FIVE:
LEARNING THROUGH CRISIS

Staying the Course: Lessons from the 2008 Crash and Market Volatility

Economic uncertainty and stock market volatility are inevitable. Throughout my years of experience, I have consistently advised those I work with to remain diligent, stay informed, and make strategic adjustments as needed. During unstable periods, a shift from high-growth stocks to more stable, value-based investments can help preserve wealth while maintaining proper diversification across all asset classes in a 401(k) portfolio.

The key is not to panic, but to adapt. A well-structured plan is designed to withstand fluctuations, and the ability to adjust your allocations while staying invested is crucial to long-term success.

Lessons from the 2008 Market Crash

One of the most significant financial crises in modern history was the 2008 market crash. No one was immune—from Wall Street to Main Street, millions of Americans saw their retirement savings and investments take massive hits. The market plummeted over **50%**, wiping out years of savings in **401(k) plans, 403(b) accounts, IRAs, brokerage accounts, and even employer-sponsored pensions.** It was a time of fear, uncertainty, and financial devastation.

I remember that period vividly because I experienced it personally. In a single day, I lost approximately **$45,000**. That moment could have been a breaking point for me, but instead of allowing fear to dictate my financial future, I **chose to adapt**. Rather than seeing it as a failure, I viewed it as an opportunity to rebuild with a new perspective. I didn't withdraw from the market. I didn't stop contributing. I stayed the course.

For many others, however, the decision was not theirs to make. People were **forced to stop contributing** due to job losses, financial hardships, or unexpected life events. I understood their circumstances, as each person and family faced unique challenges during that time. Some potential retirees saw their entire savings **wiped out overnight**, while others **lost their homes**. The crash was sudden, ruthless, and life-altering.

Staying Committed to the Plan

During times of market turbulence, it's easy to let emotions take over. But **successful investing is not about reacting impulsively; it's about making informed, strategic decisions.**

Through it all, I encouraged my colleagues and clients to remain **active participants** in their retirement planning. That didn't mean ignoring the crisis; it meant making smart adjustments while keeping their long-term vision intact. Those who could continue contributing and rebalancing their portfolios had the opportunity to recover. In fact, many who followed a disciplined approach saw their investments **fully rebound** in the years that followed, eventually reaching **new all-time highs**.

There is no magic formula or shortcut to success in investing. Building and maintaining a strong retirement plan requires:

☑ **Education** – Understanding how the market and different funds work

☑ **Discipline** – Staying consistent and avoiding emotional decisions

☑ **Adaptability** – Adjusting when needed but remaining committed to long-term goals

The Market Moves Two Ways – Be Prepared

When uncertainty arises, I remind people of a simple but critical truth:

The market only moves in two directions—up and down.

Those who recognize this and prepare accordingly will **thrive**, while those who react out of fear may struggle to regain their footing. Investing isn't about chasing quick wins; it's about playing the long game, weathering the storms, and emerging stronger on the other side.

If there's one thing I learned from 2008, it's this: **Stay informed. Stay engaged. Stay invested.** The market will always recover, and those who remain committed to their financial future will reap the benefits over time.

PART SIX:
EMPOWERING FAMILY

Helping My Sister Retire: Real-Life Lessons in Rebuilding and Recovery

Helping My Sister Build a Retirement Plan

The first person I successfully helped create and build a solid retirement plan for was my sister, Miss Transit, in **2015**. At the time, she was focused on her career and hadn't given much thought to how her retirement plan was performing. When I initially shared with her what I had learned about **401(k) investing** over the past fifteen years, she mentioned that she was already working with a financial advisor recommended by her former employer.

We didn't discuss it much then, and I assumed she was in good hands. After all, she was earning a high income, and with an advisor managing her portfolio, I expected her to be on track toward a comfortable retirement.

Fast forward six years, and we had another conversation about her financial future. She told me she planned to retire within **two years**. However, as we talked, I realized something alarming—she had not spoken with her advisor in several years, and worse, **her retirement account had significantly declined in value**.

I was shocked.

Despite working hard her entire life, she was far from reaching her financial goal, so I asked her a simple question:

"Would you let me take a look at your plan?"

She agreed, and when I reviewed her **401(k) portfolio**, I immediately saw the problem—she wasn't anywhere close to her retirement goal. In fact, she was at risk of running out of money in retirement if she continued on her current path.

The Reality Check: Overcoming Debt and Low Contributions

After digging deeper into her finances, I uncovered several key issues holding her back:

- **She had a significant amount of debt**, including loans that needed to be repaid before she could retire comfortably.
- **Her 401(k) contributions were far too low**—she wasn't even contributing enough to take full advantage of her employer's match.
- **She had been making poor investment choices**, and because she hadn't adjusted her portfolio in years, her account had lost value instead of growing.

It became clear that **retiring in two years was not an option**.

I had a serious conversation with her and told her, **"Retirement is not just about reaching a certain age—it's about having enough money to sustain your lifestyle without financial stress."**

Then I asked her the big question:

"Are you willing to work five more years before retiring?"

She hesitated. Like most people, she had a retirement date in mind, and she was emotionally attached to that goal. However, I explained that **if she was willing to adjust her timeline and commit to a structured plan, she could retire with confidence instead of uncertainty.**

She agreed. And that's when we got to work.

Building a New Plan for Success

The first step was tackling **her debt**. I developed a strategy that would allow her to **systematically eliminate her loans within three years**, focusing on high-interest debts first.

At the same time, I guided her through the process of **increasing her 401(k) contributions**. We set up a plan where she would **gradually increase her contributions over time** to maximize her savings without feeling overwhelmed.

Additionally, we reviewed her **investment allocations** and restructured them to align with her retirement goals. She had previously invested in high-risk funds that weren't serving her well, so we **diversified her portfolio** to create a balanced mix of **growth, income, and stability**.

The result?

✅ Within three years, she had completely eliminated her debt.

✅ She was consistently contributing to her 401(k) at a much higher rate than before.

✅ Her portfolio began to grow steadily, putting her back on track for a secure retirement.

By sticking to this plan, she was finally able to reach her financial goal. She officially **retired on January 1, 2020**, and has not worked a single day since.

This experience reinforced an important lesson: **Everyone's retirement plan is unique.** There is no universal number or magic formula—it all comes down to understanding your financial situation, setting clear goals, and taking deliberate steps to achieve them.

Helping Others Achieve Financial Freedom

After successfully helping my sister, I realized how many people struggle with the same challenges. I decided to extend my guidance to others and offer them the same strategies and insights I had developed over the years.

One of my most rewarding experiences was working with an **assistant basketball coach, Mack,** from my **high school alma mater**. He had been contributing to his 401(k) for years but wasn't sure if he was on the right track for retirement. Over the course of **six years**, I helped him **adjust his contributions, manage his investments, and optimize his retirement plan**. Thanks to his dedication, he was able to **retire comfortably within his target timeframe**.

Another individual I worked with—a **team leader, Mr. LongGame,** came to me as a referral from my cousin. He had been unsure about his retirement strategy and needed a clear plan to follow. After attending a few of my consultation meetings and applying my recommendations, he successfully **reached his retirement goal in just three years**.

Even today, I continue to work with people who are navigating the complexities of their **401(k) plans**. Some aim for **early retirement**, while others want to ensure they have enough financial security to enjoy their golden years.

The Power of a Well-Planned Retirement

One of the most fulfilling aspects of my work is seeing the positive impact financial planning has on people's lives.

I've seen people who were once burdened by debt finally experience financial freedom.

I've helped individuals **transition into retirement with confidence**, knowing they have the resources they need.

I've watched former clients move on to new phases in life—**starting businesses, spending more time with their families, or pursuing their passions**.

Every person I've worked with has taken a **different path**, but the one thing they all have in common is this: **They took action.** They made the choice to educate themselves, adjust their plans, and take control of their financial future.

And that's what makes all the difference.

My Purpose: Serving Others

Through these experiences, I've come to understand **why I am here—to serve others and help them improve their lives.**

It's not just about numbers, investments, or financial strategies. **It's about people.** It's about **helping individuals take control of their future and giving them the tools to live life on their own terms**.

I truly believe that financial knowledge is one of the most powerful gifts you can give someone. For me, there's no greater reward than seeing the people I've helped achieve their financial goals and enjoy the retirement they've worked so hard for.

For that, I am genuinely grateful.

PART SEVEN:
HABITS FOR SUCCESS

Consistency Over Time: Building Strong Habits for Lifelong Retirement Success

Building Strong Financial Habits for Retirement

When it comes to planning for retirement, success is not just about earning a high income—it's about making **strategic and disciplined financial decisions over time**. A well-structured 401(k) plan doesn't grow overnight, nor does it succeed based on wishful thinking. Instead, it requires **consistent habits, best practices, and a long-term mindset**.

Over the years, I have learned that the people who achieve their retirement goals are not necessarily the ones who make the most money. They are the ones who:

- ✅ **Start early and remain consistent.**
- ✅ **Maximize their employer match.**
- ✅ **Increase their contributions regularly.**
- ✅ **Reallocate their investments as needed.**
- ✅ **Stay patient and focused, even during market downturns.**

If you apply these principles, you will be well on your way to financial security.

The Power of Employer Matching Contributions

One of the **biggest mistakes** employees make is **not taking full advantage of their employer's matching contributions**.

Every employer sets their own **matching policy**. Some companies match **dollar for dollar** up to a certain percentage (such as 5%), while others may match **50 cents for every dollar** up to a specific limit.

Whatever the case may be, one rule should always apply:

✅ **Contribute at least up to your employer's full match.**

Think of employer matching as **free money**—it is essentially a **bonus** that gets invested into your retirement for simply participating in the plan.

For example:

- If your employer matches **5%** and you earn **$60,000 per year**, that's an extra **$3,000** per year in your 401(k)—at no cost to you.
- Over 30 years, with compounding, that "**free**" **$3,000 per year** could grow into a **six-figure addition to your retirement savings**.

Failing to take advantage of an **employer match is like refusing free money**, and yet **millions of employees leave thousands of dollars on the table every year** simply because they **do not contribute enough** to receive the full match.

The 90-Day Rule: Regular Plan Reviews

Once you begin contributing consistently, your next task is to **monitor and review your plan every 90 days**.

Why is this important?

✅ **Market conditions change.**
✅ **Your employer may adjust their plan options.**
✅ **You may receive a raise or bonus, which affects your contribution potential.**
✅ **Your long-term goals or risk tolerance may shift over time.**

I recommend setting a **reminder every three months** to:

📌 **Check your investment allocations.**
📌 **Review your contribution percentage.**
📌 **Ensure your beneficiaries are up to date.**
📌 **Look for any new investment options available in your plan.**

Many people ignore their **401(k) accounts for years**, only to be surprised when they realize they **haven't been contributing**

enough or that their **investments are not performing as expected**.

Taking just **30 minutes every three months** to review your account can **make a world of difference** over the span of your career.

Scaling Up Your Contributions for Maximum Growth

Once you have built a **habit of contributing consistently**, the next step is to **increase your contributions strategically**.

I recommend the **2% Rule**:

☑ **Increase your 401(k) contributions by 2% every year.**

A great way to do this is to **align contribution increases with salary raises**.

For example:

- If you receive a **2% raise**, increase your **401(k) contribution by that same 2%**.
- If you follow this approach for **10 years**, your contributions will have grown significantly—without feeling like a burden on your budget.

The **short-term goal** is to work toward contributing **at least 10% of your take-home pay** to your 401(k).

For **long-term success**, if you can **set your contribution rate to 15% and maintain it for 30 years**, you will build a **substantial retirement nest egg**.

The Power of Compounding and Long-Term Commitment

Many people **underestimate the power of compounding**.

✅ **Your investments generate returns.**
✅ **Those returns generate additional returns.**
✅ **Your account balance multiplies exponentially over time.**

For example:

- If you contribute **$500 per month** to your 401(k) and your investments grow at an **average rate of 8% annually**, your account could **grow to over $1 million** after **40 years**.

The key is **starting early and staying consistent**.

The biggest regret I hear from retirees is **"I wish I had started saving earlier."**

Employer Contributions Vary – But Your Commitment Shouldn't

Not all employers offer the same **match percentage**, and some may not provide **any match at all**.

This is why it's critical to **take full ownership of your retirement planning**.

If your employer matches only **3%**, that doesn't mean you should only contribute 3%.

✅ **Your financial future is in your hands, not your employer's.**
✅ **Make it a priority to contribute as much as you can afford.**
✅ **Remember, Social Security alone is NOT enough for retirement.**

You **must** take an **active** role in securing your financial future.

Retirement Is Your Responsibility—No One Else's

One of the **most important lessons I've learned** is this:

No one is coming to save you.

I want to make this clear:

Your employer is not responsible for your retirement.
The government is not responsible for your retirement.
Your financial advisor is not responsible for your retirement.

YOU are responsible for your retirement.

Your **future self** will either **thank you** for the financial decisions you made today—or **struggle** because of the choices you avoided.

PART EIGHT:
STRATEGIC GROWTH

My Path to a Strong 401(k): Step-by-Step Growth Through Discipline and Planning

My Personal Journey to Building a Strong 401(k) Balance

During my career in the banking industry, I was able to **amass a respectable 401(k) balance in just seven and a half years**.

My personal experience was **unique, strategic, and creative**. While this is not financial advice, I would like to share my journey as an example of how someone can fully leverage a 401(k) plan and **maximize** their retirement savings through **consistent contributions, strategic increases, and long-term planning**.

The key takeaway from my experience is simple:

Your financial future is built on the decisions you make today.

Laying the Foundation: My First Year in a 401(k) Plan

My first year participating in my employer-sponsored **401(k) plan** was eye-opening. I saw my retirement account grow by **$12,000**, thanks to a **5% dollar-for-dollar employer match**. Seeing that amount accumulate within a year made me realize the power of **consistent contributions**.

This experience encouraged me to set a personal goal: **to increase my contributions over time and build a strong retirement account.** Instead of merely relying on my employer's match, I decided to take matters into my own hands. I knew that the more I invested in my future at the time, the greater my financial security would be later.

Many employees stop contributing at just what their employer matches, but this is where most people **miss out on real growth**. Your employer's match is helpful, but your **own contributions** are what truly determine the size of your retirement fund.

A Strategic Approach: How I Increased My Contributions

After seeing the benefits of participating in my **401(k) plan**, I adopted a **progressive approach to increasing my contributions**. Each year, I boosted my percentage, which allowed my savings to grow exponentially.

Here's how I structured it:

First Year: I started with **5%**, taking full advantage of my employer's **5% dollar-for-dollar match**, ensuring I was not leaving any free money on the table.

Second Year: I increased my contribution to **7%**, slowly surpassing my employer's match.

Third Year: I raised it to **10%**, making my personal contributions double what my employer was contributing.

Fourth Year: I boosted my contribution to **12%**, further accelerating the growth of my retirement savings.

Fifth Year: I increased it to **15%**, a percentage that set me apart from most employees, who only contribute the minimum.

Sixth & Seventh Year: I reached my highest contribution level at **20%**, making my retirement savings even more powerful over time.

By gradually increasing my contributions each year, I ensured **rapid and consistent growth** without feeling a sudden financial burden.

Why Increasing Contributions Matters

A common mistake employees make is keeping their contribution percentage the same year after year. While that might feel comfortable, it **doesn't take into account inflation, salary increases, or long-term financial security**. If your employer gives you a raise, consider increasing your **401(k) contributions at the same rate**.

For example, if your employer gives you a **2% salary increase**, raising your **401(k) contribution by 2%** ensures that you're **saving more without feeling the impact** on your take-home pay. Over time, this small adjustment can make a massive difference.

Compounding interest is also a powerful tool in wealth-building. The more money you contribute early, the **more time it has to grow exponentially**. That's why delaying contributions or keeping them at a low percentage can cost you thousands (or even hundreds of thousands) over your lifetime.

Rolling Over My 401(k) to an IRA with Fidelity

When I separated from my employer, I had an important decision to make about my **401(k) and pension**. Many people leave their funds in their former employer's plan, but I knew that rolling over my retirement savings into an **IRA with Fidelity** was the best choice.

By rolling over my funds, I gained access to:

✅ **More investment options** compared to my previous employer's plan.
✅ **Lower fees**, ensuring that more of my money stayed invested and growing.

✅ **Greater control over my portfolio**, allowing me to customize my investments.

When I met with the **Fidelity financial advisor**, she reviewed my investment strategy and asked, **"Who created this plan for you?"**

I confidently told her, **"I did it myself."**

She smiled and said, **"It looks like you don't need my help."** That moment reassured me that the effort I had put into **learning and strategizing** had paid off. I had developed a **solid** and **well-diversified portfolio** that would support my retirement goals.

The Importance of Starting Now

Looking back, the biggest lesson I learned was **the importance of starting as early as possible**.

Many people believe they can delay retirement planning until later in life. However, the earlier you start, the more **compounding interest works in your favor**. Even if you begin with small contributions, consistent participation over decades leads to **significant wealth accumulation**.

The best part? **It's never too late to start.** Whether you're in your 20s, 30s, or even 40s, taking action today is better than waiting for tomorrow. The longer you wait, the **more difficult it becomes to catch up**.

Your Financial Future Is in Your Hands

One harsh reality about retirement planning is that **no one will do it for you.**

No government program will fully cover your expenses. No employer will guarantee you financial freedom.

No one will care about your future more than YOU.

That's why it's essential to **take control of your finances today**.

Action beats inaction every time. Whether it's making your first contributions, increasing your savings rate, or rolling over your funds into an IRA, every decision you make today **impacts your future financial security**.

Final Thoughts: The Power of Taking the First Step

I have continued to **actively grow my retirement portfolio for over 12 years**, using the same principles I followed from the beginning.

✅ **Consistent contributions** ensure that you're always making progress.

✅ **Strategic increases** help you take advantage of salary growth and compounding interest.

✅ **Diversified, long-term investments** provide financial stability and security.

✅ **Discipline and patience** are the keys to long-term success.

The most important step is to simply start.

You don't need to be a financial expert. You don't need to have all the answers today. You just need to **make the decision to begin**.

Because when the time comes to retire, **you'll be grateful you did.**

PART NINE:
MARKET MASTERY

Weathering the Storm: Recovering from Market Downturns with Data-Driven Decisions

Lessons Learned Through Market Volatility

Not all my experiences creating and building my 401(k) account—or the accounts of the individuals I've served—have been easy or positive. Like many others, I faced substantial setbacks during the **2008 financial crisis**. I lost an amount equivalent to a full year's salary. It was one of the most sobering moments of my career. However, what mattered most was how I responded.

Instead of panicking or abandoning my plan, I waited until the market began to stabilize. Then, I initiated a recovery strategy: For an entire year, I rebalanced my account every 30 days. I reviewed allocations monthly, made small adjustments, and consistently tracked performance. Thirteen months later, I had successfully regained what I had lost—and even earned a modest gain.

The key strategy during that time was shifting from **growth to value positions**. Growth funds tend to be aggressive and thrive in expanding markets, while value funds are more conservative and offer steadier performance in uncertain times. Balancing the two is delicate, but with education and observation, I learned to make timely adjustments that protected the portfolios I managed, including my own.

Navigating Market Corrections: Lessons from the 2022 Downturn

The **market downturn of 2022** presented many of the same challenges I had seen in previous financial crises, including the crash of 2008. However, each period of market volatility is different, and success in these environments depends not only on experience but also on real-time decision-making based on the best available information.

As the markets declined sharply and consistently throughout 2022, many investors were overwhelmed. Volatility was high, uncertainty reigned, and fear crept in quickly. In these moments, rash decisions often lead to long-term consequences—especially in retirement planning. Many fail to realize that **making adjustments while the market is falling** requires discipline, patience, and, most importantly, access to relevant, accurate data. You can't react emotionally—you must respond intelligently.

When volatility increases and markets begin to fall, **timing is critical**. There is a narrow window to reposition your portfolio into more defensive assets before deeper losses occur. Defensive positions typically include stable, income-generating investments, such as **value funds, dividend-paying stocks, or bond**

funds, which are less sensitive to economic downturns than high-growth equities.

I didn't rely on hunches or media headlines to make those adjustments effectively. I followed a **data-driven approach** grounded in key economic indicators, consistently offering insights into market direction and momentum. These include:

Federal Reserve Communications

The statements, press conferences, and policy reports released by the Federal Reserve serve as a compass for market trends. These communications shed light on future interest rate hikes or cuts, inflation targets, and the overall monetary policy stance. When the Fed signals that interest rates will continue to rise to combat inflation, it indicates that growth stocks may come under pressure. At the same time, value-oriented or fixed-income investments might offer safer ground.

Consumer Price Index (CPI) and Producer Price Index (PPI)

These two indicators measure the rate of inflation. The **CPI tracks changes in the price of goods and services** paid by consumers, while the **PPI monitors prices from the perspective of manufacturers and wholesalers**. Rising inflation pressures consumers and companies, often resulting in reduced spending and lower corporate earnings—factors that weigh heavily on equity markets. Tracking these reports monthly allowed me to anticipate when inflationary pressures were intensifying or easing.

Monthly Jobs Reports

The labor market's health is one of the most reliable indicators of economic resilience. When unemployment rises or job creation slows, consumer spending often declines—which can signal a downturn. Conversely, substantial employment numbers indicate that people are working, earning, and spending, which helps support company revenues and, by extension, the stock market. These reports helped me gauge the overall strength or weakness of the economy at any given moment.

Personal Consumption Expenditures (PCE)

The PCE report, particularly its "core" version (which excludes food and energy), is a favorite metric of the Federal Reserve for measuring inflation. It offers insight into what consumers spend money on and how inflation affects their habits. Changes in consumer behavior can be a signal of shifts in economic momentum. For instance, if consumers are cutting back on discretionary spending, this can negatively impact specific market sectors, prompting adjustments in sector exposure.

I developed an informed, structured response to the 2022 downturn using this collection of indicators. I did not attempt to time the market in a reactionary way. Instead, I identified where the market was heading and made **measured, strategic changes** to my portfolio and my clients' portfolios.

The result was a more stable position during the crash and a faster, more confident recovery as conditions improved. Rather than retreat, we rebuilt. And because we were guided by data—not fear—we could make decisions with clarity even during the most uncertain times.

Client Success Stories and Recovery Outcomes

The actual test of any financial plan is not how it performs during good times but how it holds up during periods of uncertainty. The market correction of 2022 was one of those tests—and several of my clients came through it stronger, not just financially, but also mentally and emotionally. Their stories testify to the power of strategy, trust, and unwavering commitment.

One client, whom I'll refer to as **Mr. Long-game**, exemplified these qualities. From the beginning of the downturn, he approached the situation with patience and a long-term perspective. He didn't panic when the market fell. Instead, he called, asked questions, and, most importantly, listened. We met regularly, reviewing his portfolio each quarter and making intentional, data-driven adjustments. He diligently applied every recommendation I offered and remained focused on the end goal—even when the short-term picture was discouraging. By the **fall of 2023**, not only had he recovered all the losses incurred during the downturn, but he was **fully realigned with his original retirement timeline and financial objectives**. His success was not a result of perfect timing or luck. It was earned through **disci-**

pline, trust, and willingness to adapt through every market cycle phase.

Another client, **Coach Mack**, had a very similar journey. Like Mr. Long Game, he experienced sharp declines in his retirement account in early 2022. But he didn't allow fear or frustration to guide his actions. He remained consistent, applied the strategies we discussed, and showed up month after month for our scheduled check-ins. Each meeting was an opportunity to recalibrate, discuss market movements, and reallocate where needed. His recovery was methodical, not reactionary. By the end of 2023, he had also regained his portfolio's value and was **back on a growth trajectory**, perfectly positioned for the next chapter of his retirement plan.

Beyond these two, several other clients I supported during that time experienced positive outcomes. While the details of each case varied—different careers, incomes, retirement timelines, and degrees of risk tolerance—the core behaviors remained consistent across the board. The individuals who made it through the storm successfully all practiced the same three principles:

1. **They trusted the process.**
2. **They remained consistent in their participation.**
3. **They made strategic, incremental improvements instead of emotional decisions.**

What mattered most wasn't the size of their accounts—it was their **commitment to the journey**. They believed in their plan, stayed informed, and remained engaged through every high and low. These qualities, more than anything, determined their outcome.

Embracing the Calling to Serve

These stories aren't just success cases—they are affirmations of my purpose. Each client who recovered, each portfolio that rebounded, and each family that regained hope for the future reminded me of something I have come to believe with certainty: **I was born to serve.**

This work goes far beyond numbers on a spreadsheet. It's about more than financial growth; it's about **empowerment, resilience, and transformation**. It's about taking someone from a place of uncertainty to a place of clarity—and doing it with care, patience, and integrity. I've never measured the value of my work by the dollar. I measure it by the impact it leaves behind.

Serving others in this capacity has never been about financial gain—it has always been about **making a difference**. When someone trusts you, they're not just asking for help with money—they're asking for **guidance, reassurance, and hope**. They want to know someone is walking beside them, especially when the path becomes unclear.

I've had the honor of walking that path with many individuals. I've sat across the table or behind a Zoom screen, helping people navigate layoffs, life changes, family responsibilities, and financial fear. I've celebrated their milestones—retirements, debt payoffs, first investments—and stood by them through their lowest moments.

What I've learned is this: **People don't just need a financial**

plan—they need a partner. Someone who understands the markets, yes, but also understands people. Someone who listens, teaches, and empowers.

The market will always fluctuate, and there will always be uncertainty. But with education, discipline, and consistent leadership, anyone can weather the storm.

For me, there is **no greater reward** than seeing someone reach their goal, knowing that I had the opportunity to contribute. That is my calling. That is why I do this work. And that is what continues to drive me forward—every day, with every client, through every season.

PART TEN:
EXPANDING THE VISION

Beyond the 401(k): Exploring Other Tools for Retirement Security

Setting the Vision for Retirement

Reaching financial security in retirement doesn't happen by accident—it happens by design. Once you are vested in your employer-sponsored 401(k) and have developed the habit of consistent contributions, it's time to begin setting your sights on a specific financial goal. This "retirement number" should reflect not only your expected expenses in retirement but also the lifestyle you envision living.

Everyone's number will look different. For one person, the goal may be to save $250,000 over a decade for an early retirement. For another, it may be a million-dollar portfolio accumulated over 30 years. The timeline, the amount, and the strategy will vary. The unifying principle, however, is that **you need to define your goal clearly and pursue it consistently**.

Consider this practical example: If you earn $50,000 annually and commit to contributing 5% of your salary—roughly $205 per month—you're already taking powerful steps toward long-term financial health. Combine this with a 5% employer match that doubles your contribution, and over time, with the power of compound interest, this seemingly modest amount can grow into a substantial sum. The most important decision you can make is to **pay yourself first**. Treat your retirement savings like a non-negotiable expense, like your mortgage or utility bill.

Exploring Life After the 401(k)

A well-funded 401(k) is a powerful tool, but it's not the only one. Once you've gained confidence and traction with your employer plan, it's essential to look beyond it and develop a more comprehensive strategy for long-term wealth preservation and income generation.

There are several financial vehicles designed to help you supplement your 401(k) and enhance your retirement readiness:

- **Individual Retirement Accounts (IRAs)** are among the most commonly used. A Traditional IRA allows for tax-deferred growth, while a Roth IRA offers the advantage of tax-free withdrawals in retirement. Both provide flexibility and investment options beyond what many employer plans offer.
- **Annuities** provide guaranteed income for life or a set period, often used by retirees to protect against outliving their savings. They can be fixed or variable and are usually funded by rolling over retirement assets.

- **Universal Life Insurance and Whole Life Insurance** policies serve dual purposes: life coverage and cash value accumulation. These products can offer access to funds through loans or withdrawals and are helpful in estate planning or as alternative savings tools.
- **Roth IRAs and other tax-free investment accounts** can offer significant advantages for those looking to manage their tax liability in retirement. When used strategically, these accounts can help protect your savings from future tax increases.

These tools aren't one-size-fits-all, so understanding how each option fits into your unique financial picture is key. They allow you to diversify your retirement strategy, hedge against market risks, and position yourself to achieve financial peace of mind.

Seeking Professional Guidance

As you accumulate wealth and move closer to retirement, navigating the financial landscape becomes more complex. During this stage, a financial professional's guidance can be invaluable. A trusted advisor or planner will help you evaluate your current position, understand your options, and develop strategies that align with your goals.

However, not all advisors are created equally, and not all approaches are in your best interest. That's why it's essential to approach these conversations with a set of specific, informed questions:

1. **What products and services do you offer that align with my goals?** Ask for clear explanations. You want to know whether the advisor offers proprietary products or a wide array of market-based options.
2. **How can I roll over my 401(k) without triggering taxes or penalties?** This is essential if you're considering a move to an IRA or another retirement vehicle. A proper rollover should be tax-deferred and penalty-free when done correctly.
3. **What are your fees, and how are they structured?** Transparency is critical. Are they commission-based or fee-only? You want to know how they are compensated and how that may influence their advice.
4. **How can I protect my account against market crashes?** Market downturns are inevitable. You should have a plan that includes asset allocation strategies and risk management tools to weather financial storms.
5. **Can I access funds in case of emergencies?** Life happens. Whether it's a medical expense, a family crisis, or an opportunity, you want to understand the rules for hardship withdrawals, loans, or partial distributions—and the associated costs.

Asking these questions doesn't just keep you informed—it keeps you **in control**. You've worked hard to build your retirement plan. It's your right and responsibility to protect it.

The Road to Financial Freedom

Financial freedom is not a destination—it's a journey. It's achieved through **daily, weekly, and monthly decisions** over years of dedication and sacrifice. It's the result of every budget you created, every contribution you made, every market report you read, and every time you chose not to give up. This journey is not linear. There will be ups and downs, periods of growth, and moments of uncertainty. However, the rewards are transformational if you stay the course with discipline and intention.

As I reflect on my own journey, which began more than twenty years ago in the banking industry, I now see it as more than just a job—it was a calling. I didn't start out knowing I'd end up here, but in hindsight, every challenge I faced and every person I helped was leading me toward a higher purpose.

We are all called to serve in different ways. For me, service has come in **education, empowerment, and encouragement**—guiding people toward a clearer financial future. This isn't just about managing money; it's about changing lives, restoring confidence, and showing others what's possible when they take ownership of their financial future.

Yes, the road to retirement can be intimidating. It can feel overwhelming at times, but it can also be rewarding, liberating, and deeply fulfilling. Financial planning is not a burden—it is a privilege and an opportunity to honor your hard work by making thoughtful decisions about the future you want to live.

So if you're reading this and haven't started yet, let me remind you: **You don't have to have it all figured out—you have to begin.** The most powerful step in any journey is the first one.

Start now. Your future depends on it.

PART ELEVEN:
LESSONS IN TRUST

A Painful Mistake: Losing Half My 401(k) and Learning to Take Control

Your 401(k) Is Just a Click Away – Expanded

In 1999, my family and I embarked on a new chapter of our lives. We had moved to South Texas only a year prior, still adjusting to the rhythms of a new community and culture. At that time, we focused on settling down, raising a family, and building a life in an unfamiliar territory. In many ways, we were just beginning to map out our future—both personally and financially.

Shortly after settling into our new jobs and routines, my wife and I began the search for our first home. As newcomers, we leaned heavily on referrals and guidance from locals. A financial advisor who had reached out to us upon our arrival mentioned that his family had experience in real estate. Given our lack of knowledge about the local market, we welcomed the help.

To his credit, he and his family helped us with our first home purchase. That positive experience built a level of trust that we didn't question at the time. Encouraged by the results of our real estate journey, we decided to extend our trust even further—we turned to him for guidance on our retirement investments.

In hindsight, that decision would become one of the costliest financial lessons of my life.

A Costly Lesson in Trust and Oversight – Expanded

Approximately a year and a half after purchasing our home, we received an unexpected call from the advisor's office. The news that followed was both shocking and disheartening. My wife's retirement account had been completely depleted—100% gone. My account suffered a substantial blow, losing nearly 50% of its value.

Confused and alarmed, I reviewed our statements and immediately visited the advisor's office to understand what had happened. When I asked why we weren't notified earlier or given any indication that the market was affecting our accounts so drastically, his response was dismissive. He said, "You should've been paying attention to the market and the economy."

That response revealed a deep misunderstanding of his role—not only as a financial advisor but as someone entrusted with our future. I explained to him that I was not an investor or market analyst. Like many working professionals, I had sought the expertise of a licensed advisor to help protect and grow our retirement funds. Instead, I had received no updates, warnings, or strategies—just silence.

Both my wife and I were devastated. We had made responsible decisions: We worked, saved, and trusted. Yet, despite all of that, we were now forced to confront an unexpected financial loss due to negligence and a lack of communication. I immediately withdrew what remained of my account and safeguarded the funds elsewhere.

This experience, though painful, would eventually serve as a turning point. It happened nearly three years before I began my career in financial services, but it planted the seed for everything that followed.

Taking Ownership of My Financial Future – Expanded

That event, as traumatic as it was, changed the course of my thinking forever. I made a firm and personal vow: **Never again would I allow someone else to control my financial future without accountability.**

From then on, I committed to learning investing principles, studying the markets, and developing a hands-on approach to managing my retirement. Over the next two decades, I applied those lessons with consistency and care. I became the one reviewing statements. I became the one making decisions, and eventually, I taught others how to avoid the same mistakes I had made.

This experience didn't make me bitter—it made me better. While I still believe that financial advisors have a valuable role to play, clients must remain engaged. Blind trust without oversight can be dangerous. Advisors should be held to a high communication, transparency, and responsibility standard.

I now encourage everyone—especially those beginning their

retirement journey—to ask the hard questions. Don't be intimidated. This is your money; no one should ever manage it without your understanding and consent.

Ask your advisor:

- How often will you review my account?
- What's your investment philosophy?
- How do you respond to market volatility?
- What protections do I have in place?

If you don't receive thoughtful answers, keep asking—or consider moving on.

Your Responsibility, Your Future – Expanded

The good news is that today's technology makes it easier than ever to stay involved. Most employer-sponsored retirement plans offer user-friendly dashboards, performance reports, and mobile access. You no longer have to wait for a quarterly paper statement to know where you stand. Your **401(k) is really just a click away.**

I advise everyone I coach to treat their retirement account like their most important financial relationship. Log in regularly, review your investments, and monitor performance. If something doesn't look right, ask. If you need clarification, seek help. Passive participation leads to missed opportunities, while active engagement leads to growth, confidence, and long-term success.

That experience 26 years ago helped me discover my life's purpose. It was the beginning of my journey into financial literacy and financial leadership. It was the moment I realized that **no one will ever care about my money more than I do**—and that's true for you too.

The road to retirement is paved with daily decisions. Don't leave yours to chance. Take ownership. Ask questions. Stay involved. And above all, remember that **financial freedom is not a destination—it's a mindset**.

It is worth telling this story if it helps even one person avoid a similar mistake. If you've never looked at your 401(k) account, let today be the day you log in, review your goals, and take one step closer to building the secure future you deserve.

PART TWELVE:
FULL CIRCLE

Understanding the 401(k): The Final Step in Building a Secure Future

Understanding the Foundation: What Is a 401(k) Plan?

Before you can fully appreciate the power of a 401(k), it's important to understand what it is—and what it is not. At its core, a 401(k) plan is more than just a workplace benefit. It is a structured, tax-advantaged retirement account that gives individuals the opportunity to invest consistently over time toward their future financial independence.

As defined by **Investopedia**, a 401(a) plan—a close relative of the 401(k)—is an **employer-sponsored, money-purchase retirement plan** that allows for **either dollar-based or percentage-based contributions** from the employer, the employee, or both. The sponsoring employer is responsible for establishing the **eligibility rules** and **vesting schedule**, which determine how and when employees acquire full ownership of the funds contributed on their behalf.

In practical terms, this means that as an employee, you're

able to participate in a structured plan where your employer helps you save for retirement, often by contributing a matching percentage of your salary into your 401(k) account. This is frequently referred to as "**free money**" because it is money your employer offers to invest on your behalf, provided you contribute as well.

Over time, those contributions—your own and your employer's—are invested into a variety of financial vehicles, such as mutual funds, index funds, or target-date funds. These investments are chosen based on your preferences, risk tolerance, and retirement timeline. The real value of a 401(k) lies in its ability to **grow tax-deferred**, which means you don't pay taxes on earnings until you withdraw the money in retirement. If managed well, this tax advantage can lead to significantly higher growth over the decades.

Vesting, Portability, and Withdrawal Options

Another critical feature of the 401(k)—or any defined contribution plan—is **vesting**. Vesting determines how much of the employer's contributions you get to keep if you leave your job. Some companies offer **immediate vesting**, while others implement **graded schedules**, which may require several years of service before you're entitled to the full match.

Equally important is understanding your **withdrawal options**. When leaving an employer, you are not forced to leave your 401(k) behind. Instead, you may choose to **roll over** your funds into another qualified retirement plan, such as an Individual Retirement Account (IRA), or into your new employer's plan if permitted. This process allows you to continue your investment strategy without tax penalties, provided it is done correctly.

Employees may also opt for a **lump-sum distribution** or convert their savings into an **annuity** that provides guaranteed income during retirement. Each option carries specific tax implications and must be carefully weighed in light of your financial goals, income needs, and risk profile.

Why This Knowledge Matters

This foundational knowledge of how retirement plans work is not only empowering—it is essential. Too many people begin contributing to a 401(k) without truly understanding what the plan offers, how to access its benefits, or how to grow their savings strategically.

Throughout this book, I've shared personal experiences—some filled with growth and others marked by hard lessons. What I've learned through it all is that **understanding the mechanics of your retirement plan gives you control over your financial destiny**. Whether you are just starting or nearing the end of your career, the decisions you make today will shape the future you experience tomorrow.

Learning what a 401(k) is, how vesting works, what your rollover options are, and how your investments perform over time isn't just good advice—it's a financial necessity.

A Final Word of Thanks

Thank you for joining me on this journey. I hope that the lessons shared throughout these chapters not only inform you but also inspire you to take action. Whether your goals are modest or ambitious, whether you're in your first job or preparing for retirement, the path to financial freedom is built one step at a time.

And remember—**it all begins with the first step.** Start today. Stay consistent. And never stop learning.

Sincerely,
Rodney McNeil

PART THIRTEEN:
THE TRANSITION AND THE CONCLUSION

Life After the 401(k): Transitioning, Reflecting, and Owning Your Financial Future

Planning for the Next Chapter: What Comes After Separation

At some point in your journey, whether through retirement or a change in employment, you will be faced with a critical decision: **What do I do with my 401(k) now that I've left my employer?**

This transition can be both exciting and daunting. You've spent years—possibly decades—building your retirement savings. Now, you must decide how to protect, preserve, and position that money for the future. The decisions you make at this point can significantly influence your long-term financial well-being.

When you leave an employer, you generally have four primary options for your retirement savings:

1. Leave the money in your former employer's 401(k) plan (if permitted).

2. Roll the money over into your new employer's plan (if available).
3. Roll the money into an Individual Retirement Account (IRA).
4. Take a lump-sum distribution.

Each option has benefits and risks, but for many individuals, the **rollover IRA** stands out as the most flexible and tax-efficient choice.

What Happens If You Leave Your Funds with Your Former Employer

Some employers will allow you to leave your retirement savings in their 401(k) plan after separation. This might seem like the easiest solution—do nothing and leave the funds where they are. However, this passive approach may not always serve your best interest.

Leaving your money with a former employer means:

- You are subject to that plan's investment offerings, which may be limited.
- You may not have direct communication with the plan administrator.
- You could lose track of the account over time, especially if your former employer is acquired, rebranded, or changes plan providers.

Additionally, since you're no longer an active employee, you may miss out on updates, newsletters, or advisory services provided to current staff. You become a passive participant in your own future—and that is rarely the best approach when it comes to your financial security.

This is why it's essential to ask your **Human Resources Department or Plan Administrator** about your options before leaving your employer. Understand the timeline, fees, and restrictions tied to leaving your funds in place.

Why the Lump-Sum Option Often Costs You More Than You Think

At first glance, receiving a large sum of money when you retire or leave your job may feel rewarding. But beware: Choosing to cash out your 401(k) in a lump sum can be one of the most financially damaging decisions you make.

If you take a lump-sum distribution before rolling over your retirement plan, you are likely to incur:

- **Federal and state income taxes**, which may be as high as 38% to 41%.
- **Early withdrawal penalties** if you are under the age of 59½.
- The potential loss of years' worth of tax-deferred growth.

Let's look at a simple example:

Suppose you've accumulated **$500,000** in your 401(k) account. If you choose to take that money as a lump sum and your combined state and federal tax rate is **38%**, you will immediately lose **$190,000** to taxes.

That leaves you with just **$310,000**—a devastating reduction that may severely impact your ability to retire comfortably. You've worked hard to build this nest egg. Why sacrifice such a significant portion of it?

The Rollover IRA: A Smart, Strategic Move

A **rollover IRA (Individual Retirement Account)** is a powerful tool for anyone leaving an employer-sponsored plan. By rolling over your 401(k) into an IRA, you maintain the tax-deferred status of your savings and gain greater flexibility in managing your investments.

Benefits of a rollover IRA include:

- **A wider range of investment options**, such as stocks, bonds, ETFs, mutual funds, and more.
- **Lower fees**, depending on the financial institution you choose.
- **No taxes or penalties** if the rollover is handled correctly.
- **Control and customization**, allowing you to align your portfolio with your personal goals and risk tolerance.

Unlike an employer-sponsored plan, a self-directed IRA gives you the freedom to make decisions and work with the providers and platforms that best fit your needs. This becomes especially important in retirement, when income planning and risk management are top priorities.

Introducing the "Four Legs of the Stool" Retirement Strategy

When managing a rollover or planning your retirement withdrawals, I use what I call the **Four Legs of the Stool Strategy**. Each "leg" represents a key component that stabilizes and supports your retirement plan.

1. **Liquidity:** This leg includes easily accessible cash reserves, such as savings or money market accounts. Liquidity is essential for handling emergencies, covering short-term needs, or avoiding the need to sell investments during market downturns.
2. **Growth Investments:** This leg is designed to provide continued growth and help combat inflation. It may include index funds, mutual funds, or diversified equity portfolios. While riskier than other components, these assets can help extend the life of your portfolio.
3. **Income-Producing Assets:** This leg includes fixed-income investments like bonds, dividend-paying stocks, or annuities. These provide predictable cash flow to meet living expenses and create stability in your portfolio.
4. **Protection Strategies:** This final leg represents insurance products, guaranteed income vehicles, or

conservative assets meant to preserve your principal. It is especially important during volatile markets or economic downturns.

When all four legs are in place, your retirement portfolio is well-balanced, providing stability, flexibility, and peace of mind.

Avoiding Common Retirement Pitfalls

One of the most overlooked aspects of transitioning into retirement is the **loss of a regular paycheck**. Once you stop working, your income becomes fixed and, in most cases, **drops by approximately 20% or more** compared to your working years.

This shift can be jarring. Your expenses may not decrease at the same rate, especially if you are still paying a mortgage, supporting children or grandchildren, or dealing with rising healthcare costs. That's why it's critical to understand how your retirement accounts will supplement your income and create a **sustainable withdrawal plan**.

Common mistakes to avoid include:

- Taking withdrawals too early or too aggressively.
- Failing to diversify across asset classes.
- Ignoring inflation and rising healthcare costs.
- Not reviewing your plan regularly.

Retirement is not a "set it and forget it" phase. You must remain engaged, informed, and flexible.

Stay In Control: Be the Captain of Your Financial Vessel

Throughout this book, we've talked about the importance of consistency, discipline, and education. Those principles don't end when you retire—they become more important than ever.

You are the captain of your financial vessel. You chart the course, adjust the sails, and make the decisions that impact your future. That means staying informed about your options, diversified in your investments, and connected to your financial plan.

Meet with your advisor regularly. Review your allocations. Track your spending. And most importantly, never abdicate control of your money to someone who doesn't have your best interest at heart.

If you choose to work with a retirement planner or advisor, ensure they are transparent, communicative, and committed to your goals. The right advisor can be a valuable partner—but you must still take responsibility for the direction of your plan.

The Final Step: Reflect, Refocus, Reclaim

Reflecting on my own journey, I recognize that every lesson I've learned—whether from success or hardship—has shaped my philosophy around retirement planning. From personal investment losses to years of advising others, I've come to understand that the most powerful strategy anyone can adopt is **intentionality**.

Be intentional with your savings. Be intentional with your investments. Be intentional with your decisions.

The First Step is not just about opening a 401(k)—it's about stepping into a new mindset, one where you own your financial future. Whether you are five years from retirement or five weeks into your first job, your ability to plan, adapt, and act will determine the outcome.

This is your journey. Make it count.

PART FOURTEEN:
THE FIRST STEP – PATIENCE AND PASSION

How to Save with a 401(k) Investing Plan

Discovering the Gap in Financial Literacy

Over the past two decades, I have worked closely with countless individuals participating in employer-sponsored retirement plans—401(k)s, 403(b)s, and TSPs (Thrift Savings Plans). In all that time, one theme has remained constant: **Very few people truly understand how to maximize the full benefits of these retirement vehicles**. Ironically, even within the organizations that offer these plans, benefits administrators rarely provide the education employees need to manage their accounts confidently.

Instead, most employees are steered toward a **"managed plan"**—a program in which a financial services team selects and monitors investments on behalf of the employee. While these services may be convenient, they often remove the opportunity for employees to take control of their financial future. What's missing is education, engagement, and empowerment.

When I first entered the workforce and explored the managed plan route, I took the time to read through all the disclosures, instructions, and performance expectations. After a month of passive engagement, I made a different choice—I turned back to my employer's benefits portal and began exploring the tools and resources available to me. I wanted to learn how to direct my plan, make informed decisions, and create a strategy for long-term success.

That decision changed everything.

Why Early Participation Matters

If you're fortunate enough to have access to a 401(k) through your employer, the smartest thing you can do is **start early and contribute consistently**. Compound interest is one of the most powerful financial forces available to you, but it requires time and commitment.

Consider this data: According to Vanguard's 2024 "How America Saves" report, the average 401(k) balance for participants aged 65 and older is $272,588. However, the **median balance**—a more realistic snapshot of the average American—is just **$88,488**. That gap represents the difference between those who start early, contribute consistently, and stay informed, and those who delay, under-contribute, or disengage.

And while Social Security offers some support, averaging $22,924 annually at age 65, it is not enough to replace a full salary. Most retirees face an income shortfall. That's why your 401(k) contributions matter so much. The more you contribute while working, the more independence and stability you'll enjoy later in life.

THE AVERAGE 401(K) BALANCE BY AGE

Age	Average Balance	Median Balance
Younger than 25	$7,351	$2,816
25 to 34	$37,557	$14,933
35 to 44	$91,281	$35,537
45 to 54	$168,646	$60,763
55 to 64	$244,750	$87,571
65 and older	$272,588	$88,488

The Motley Fool

Source: https://linktr.ee/fittipaldioffroad

Getting Started: Step by Step

If you're unsure where to begin, start with your **Human Resources Department** or **Benefits Administrator**. Ask them the following questions:

1. **How do I enroll in the company's 401(k) plan?**
2. **What is the employer's matching contribution policy?**
3. **What tools or resources are available to help me manage my account?**

Once you're enrolled, you'll need to create a **username and password** to access your retirement dashboard. This is your gateway to financial planning. Log in regularly. Review the available options. And take the time to understand how each part of the platform works.

Think of each contribution you make as **paying yourself first**. No one else is going to build your retirement plan for you. It's your responsibility—and it's your opportunity.

Understanding Investment Options

Most employer-sponsored plans include a range of investment options, typically pre-selected for their simplicity and broad coverage. These options usually include:

- **Target Date Funds** (e.g., 2030, 2040, 2050)—based on your estimated retirement year.
- **Stock or Growth Funds**—generally aggressive investments tied to market indices like the NASDAQ or Dow Jones.
- **Bond or Value Funds**—more conservative and defensive, focusing on income overgrowth.
- **Balanced or Blended Funds**—diversified across stocks and bonds, often mirroring the S&P 500.
- **Index Funds**—track the performance of a specific index or market sector.
- **Stable Funds and Money Market Funds**—designed to preserve capital with minimal risk.

When you invest in a 401(k), your money is typically placed into mutual funds or exchange-traded funds (ETFs) that hold a variety of stocks. These stocks fall into specific categories known as **sectors**—broad groupings of companies that operate in similar industries. Understanding these sectors can help you make informed decisions about how to diversify your portfolio and reduce risk.

Here's a closer look at the **11 core sectors of the stock market** and what each one represents:

1. Information Technology

This sector includes companies involved in the development of software, hardware, semiconductors, and other technologies. Think of firms like Apple, Microsoft, Nvidia, and Intel. These companies are typically high-growth and innovation-driven, making them popular in many 401(k) growth and tech-focused funds.

2. Financials

This sector includes banks, insurance companies, brokerage firms, and mortgage lenders. Companies like JPMorgan Chase, Goldman Sachs, and Bank of America operate here. Financials often do well in a strong economy and may provide dividend income, making them a solid option for income-focused investors.

3. Health Care

Comprising pharmaceutical companies, biotechnology firms, medical equipment manufacturers, and health service providers, this sector includes giants like Johnson & Johnson, Pfizer, and UnitedHealth Group. It is often considered a defensive sector because people need health care regardless of economic conditions.

4. Consumer Discretionary

This sector features companies that sell non-essential goods and services—products consumers typically buy with disposable income. Examples include Amazon, Nike, and Tesla. These stocks tend to be more cyclical and perform well when the economy is growing.

5. Communication Services

This sector includes telecommunications, media, entertainment, and internet companies. Notable players include Google's parent company Alphabet, Meta (Facebook), and Verizon. As technology and communication converge, this sector has seen rapid growth and transformation.

6. Industrials

Industrial companies manufacture goods and provide services related to construction, defense, aerospace, and machinery. Firms like Boeing, Caterpillar, and General Electric are included here. These businesses tend to be cyclical, performing well during economic expansion phases.

7. Consumer Staples

Unlike consumer discretionary, these companies sell essential products like food, beverages, and household goods. Examples include Procter & Gamble, Coca-Cola, and Walmart. Because people continue to buy these items even in downturns, this is considered a “defensive” sector.

8. Energy

This sector comprises oil, gas, and renewable energy companies. Chevron, ExxonMobil, and NextEra Energy are key players. Energy stocks can be volatile due to fluctuating commodity prices, but they are vital to the global economy and often provide dividend income.

9. Utilities

Utility companies provide electricity, natural gas, and water. Examples include Duke Energy and Dominion Energy. These stocks are considered stable and defensive, offering regular income through dividends. They are especially appealing to conservative investors or those nearing retirement.

10. Materials

This sector includes companies that produce or process raw materials—like metals, chemicals, lumber, and construction materials. Think of firms like Dow, Newmont Corporation (mining), and International Paper. Materials are closely tied to manufacturing and construction cycles.

11. Real Estate

Real estate investment trusts (REITs) and other property-related companies fall under this sector. These firms own, manage, or finance real estate assets such as commercial buildings, apartments, and warehouses. Examples include American Tower and Public Storage. REITs often pay consistent dividends and can provide a hedge against inflation.

Why These Sectors Matter to Your 401(k)

Each of these sectors behaves differently depending on the state of the economy, interest rates, inflation, and other factors. Understanding what these sectors represent can give you a better grasp of how your money is working inside your 401(k). Diversifying your investments across several sectors helps reduce risk, as a downturn in one area (like energy or financials) may be offset by gains in another (such as health care or technology).

Most 401(k) plans already offer pre-diversified mutual funds or target-date funds that span several sectors, but knowing how these funds are constructed will empower you to ask better questions, make smarter allocations, and adjust your plan as you move through your career.

How to Rebalance and Reallocate Your Investments

Over time, market performance will naturally shift the balance of your portfolio. That's why it's important to **rebalance**—periodically adjusting your investment percentages to maintain your target allocation.

Here's how to do it:

1. Log in to your retirement account and navigate to the Manage My Investments" or "Change Allocations" section of your plan dashboard.

2. Review your current asset allocation. Take note of how your funds are distributed across various investment categories—such as large-cap stocks, small-cap stocks, bonds, and cash equivalents.

3. Evaluate your risk tolerance and goals. Are you aiming for growth, income, or preservation of capital? Your age, retirement horizon, and financial needs will guide your decisions.

4. Reallocate your funds by assigning percentage values to each investment option. These must total 100%. Consider combining aggressive growth funds with more stable options like bond or balanced funds for long-term stability.

5. Submit your changes and confirm the reallocation. Most platforms will show you a summary before final submission.

This process, when done regularly, helps **protect gains, reduce risk, and maintain alignment with your overall retirement strategy**. I recommend doing this **quarterly or at least twice a year**.

Developing Financial Awareness and Market Insight

I'll be honest—this process didn't come easily at first. Learning to manage a 401(k) without a professional advisor requires not only patience but a genuine willingness to understand the financial world. Over the years, I taught myself how to read market signals and interpret economic data. I studied how global, political, and social events influence interest rates, inflation, and investor behavior.

I tuned in to:

- **Federal Reserve announcements**
- **Consumer Price Index (CPI) and Producer Price Index (PPI) reports**
- **Employment and wage data**
- **Geopolitical developments**
- **Sector-specific trends**

All of this helped me understand how to position and reposition my portfolio based on economic shifts. I also used historical fund charts—often showing 1-, 5-, or 10-year performance trends—to assess the long-term reliability and volatility of each fund.

This information may seem overwhelming at first. But in reality, it's a matter of investing time and focus. I dedicated **1 to 2 hours each month—just one day out of 365—to manage my money**. That small effort, done consistently over time, has made a significant difference.

Teaching Others Through Personal Experience

Over the years, I've developed a personal system that allows me to teach others what I've learned. My work today includes **consulting and educating individuals on how to build and grow their retirement plans**, especially self-directed accounts that do not rely on external advisors or firm-managed solutions.

Self-directed plans put the power back into the hands of the account owner. They require responsibility, but they also allow for full customization and control. With a little education, anyone can learn to manage their 401(k) effectively.

Pension plans, on the other hand, are typically **externally managed** and often funded by employers without input from the employee. These are less common today and not always flexible. While pensions may provide lifetime income, they usually do not offer the same growth potential or transparency that a well-managed 401(k) can deliver.

Patience and Passion: The Two Pillars of Success

What I've learned through my journey is that building a strong retirement plan is not about being a financial expert—it's about being **consistent, curious, and committed**. The two qualities that have sustained me are **patience and passion**.

- **Patience**, because financial education and portfolio growth take time.
- **Passion**, because helping others understand their power to control their financial future is deeply fulfilling.

The excitement I feel each time I help someone rebalance their account or meet a savings goal is very real. Watching people begin to believe in themselves, take action, and see the results reminds me of why I started on this path in the first place.

This work has never felt like a job. It's something I enjoy. It's part of who I am. And it's why I continue to teach, consult, and support others. I've walked this path myself, and now I help others walk it too—with clarity, confidence, and purpose.

Final Thoughts

If you've made it to this point in the book, I want to leave you with this final message: **You don't need to be an expert to take control of your financial future. You just need to start**. Be patient. Stay engaged. Ask questions. Learn from mistakes. And above all, commit to your goals.

A 401(k) is more than a retirement account—it's a tool to build the life you want beyond your working years. With discipline, education, and consistency, you can transform your savings into lasting security.

So log in. Review your plan. Contribute. Ask your HR department for help if you're unsure where to begin. Just take that first step.

Because the future you're building depends on what you do today.

Sincerely, **Rodney McNeil** Author / Customer

PART FIFTEEN:

MY REVELATIONS: PURPOSE, PATIENCE, AND PERSONAL GROWTH

A Journey Beyond Numbers

As I sit and reflect on this journey, one truth continues to echo in my heart: **This has been far more than a financial mission—it has been a spiritual calling, a personal transformation, and a lifetime lesson in purpose**. Over the past twenty years, I've learned that what begins as a practical need—to save for retirement—can quickly evolve into something much deeper.

This book, and the work behind it, is a product of my own lived experience. The lessons, strategies, and principles I've shared were not simply studied from textbooks—they were learned on the front lines of life, through seasons of uncertainty, growth, and revelation. And most importantly, they were **given to me by God**, who guided me through every chapter, every loss, every gain, and every new understanding.

The Measure of True Wealth

In a world that often defines success by income, position, or possessions, I've come to understand that **true wealth is not in**

what you hold—but in what you give. At the end of our lives, none of us will be remembered for the size of our 401(k) balance, but rather for the lives we touched, the wisdom we shared, and the legacy we left behind.

Service is the highest form of greatness.

And I know—without question—that I was born to serve. God placed that in me long before I knew what form it would take. For years, I thought my career in engineering was the path. But then financial literacy found me—or rather, God led me to it. I learned to speak the language of numbers so I could teach others how to listen. I became a vessel for helping people navigate something that most find intimidating and confusing.

This is my purpose—and I honor it.

Humility in Teaching and Learning

One of the great joys of this work is the opportunity to meet people from all walks of life. Over the years, I've sat across from clients, coworkers, and community members, each with different stories, challenges, and goals. And here's what I've discovered: **I've never had a conversation that didn't teach me something**.

Even as a teacher, I remain a student.

I've studied the markets, learned to interpret economic signals, and taught hundreds of people how to manage their 401(k)s—but I never assume I know everything. The moment you stop learning is the moment you start falling behind. So I remain open, curious, and humble.

A Simple Truth About the Market

People often ask me if now is a good time to invest. My answer is always rooted in the same truth: **The market moves up over time**. It does not go straight up, and it certainly doesn't rise every day—but over decades, the upward trend is clear and consistent.

There will be dips. There will be corrections. There will be crashes. But there will also be recoveries, rebounds, and records broken. What matters is your mindset. **If you approach your 401(k) with discipline and long-term thinking, you will win.**

And unlike buying individual stocks, your 401(k) is designed to help you **learn diversification, allocation, and risk management**. It's your classroom. It's your training ground. It's your introduction to how wealth is built—steadily, consistently, and patiently.

The Power of Staying Committed

I often tell clients, "If you just keep going, you'll surprise yourself."

And it's true. The power of staying consistent—of contributing to your plan month after month, year after year—cannot be overstated. Over time, your account will begin to show signs of growth. Your dividends will compound. Your balances will climb. And one day, you'll look back and be amazed at what your discipline created.

But it only works if you stay committed. This isn't about quick results; it's about lasting impact. Your retirement plan is not just a safety net—it's **a reflection of your values, your foresight, and your willingness to prioritize your future self**.

The Foundation of Financial Literacy

Financial literacy is not optional; it is essential. And yet, it remains one of the most under-taught and under-emphasized topics in our society. That's why I made it my mission not only to manage my own money but to teach others how to manage theirs.

In my business, I emphasize **education, not just execution**. I don't want clients to follow instructions blindly—I want them to understand what they're doing, why it matters, and how it works. That's how confidence is built. That's how independence is born.

I ask my clients to meet with me once a month. We spend one to two hours reviewing their plan, discussing current events, exploring new tools, and building their knowledge step by step. We walk through five clear stages of growth:

- **Year One**: Contributions—Learning the power of paying yourself first.
- **Year Two**: Diversification—Understanding how to spread risk and build balance.
- **Year Three**: Compounding—Recognizing how growth and dividends work together.
- **Year Four**: Stacking—Strategically increasing positions to build momentum.

- **Year Five**: Long-Term Planning—Setting your sights on goals and legacy.

RM Chart LLC: My Platform to Serve

Through my company, **RM Chart LLC**, and our website, www.chartdrivegroup.com, I continue this mission every day with dedication, focus, and a servant's heart. The foundation of my business isn't built on flashy sales pitches or complicated financial jargon—it's built on one guiding principle: **empower people to take ownership of their financial future**.

At RM Chart LLC, I offer **free 30-minute consultations** to individuals who are seeking clarity about their retirement plans, especially their employer-sponsored 401(k)s and 403(b)s. These sessions are not pressure-filled appointments or promotional meetings. They are honest conversations, tailored to meet people where they are.

I begin by listening. I want to understand your unique situation: What are your financial goals? Where do you currently stand with your retirement savings? Are you unsure about your plan options? Do you feel lost navigating your employer's benefits portal? Or maybe you're just starting out and need someone to guide you step by step. Wherever you are, I meet you there, with no judgment, only support.

From there, we begin developing a roadmap. Whether it's choosing the right investment allocations, learning how to diversify your holdings, understanding the importance of rebalancing, or preparing for a future rollover, my goal is always the same: **to**

educate, empower, and equip you to manage your plan with confidence.

What sets RM Chart apart is that we are **not product-driven**. I don't sell mutual funds, insurance plans, or commission-based services. Instead, **my business is built on trust, transparency, and transformation**. My success is measured not by how many clients I sign, but by how many people walk away with a greater sense of ownership and clarity over their finances.

I've worked with school teachers, corporate professionals, military veterans, healthcare workers, and small business owners. From recent graduates to those nearing retirement, each individual I serve brings a different story, but they all share the same desire: to feel prepared for the next chapter of life.

RM Chart LLC was born out of a calling, not a career strategy. It's the platform through which I live out my purpose. And as I continue to grow the business, I remain committed to making financial literacy more accessible, practical, and personal for anyone who's willing to learn.

This work is not just a business; it's a ministry. And every person I help is not just a client; they are a soul I've been called to serve.

A Call to Action: Your Future Is in Your Hands

I wrote this book for you, the person who wants to take control of their future. The person who's tired of feeling unsure about money. The person who knows they need to do more but doesn't know where to begin.

Start here. Start now. Start with one small step.

Say a prayer. Trust God. And remember this truth: **You are the creator of your backup plan**. If you're looking around, waiting for someone else to fix it, help isn't on the way. But that's not a reason to fear; it's a reason to act.

Because the moment you take ownership, everything changes.

You become the hero in your own story. You begin to walk with purpose. And every time you contribute to your plan, every time you check your dashboard, every time you learn a little more, you move closer to the future you deserve.

Final Reflections

This book has been my way of pouring into others the way God has poured into me. It's more than a guide; it's a testimony. A testimony of what's possible when we follow our calling, commit to our goals, and choose to serve others with love and wisdom.

You don't have to be perfect. You don't have to have it all figured out. You just have to begin.

So here's my challenge to you:

- Don't delay.
- Don't wait for someone else to do it for you.
- Don't give up when it gets hard.

Just start. Stay the course. And walk in faith.

Your future is waiting. Your legacy is forming. And your purpose is unfolding.

One step at a time.

Sincerely,

Rodney McNeil

Author | Educator | Financial Literacy Advocate

www.ingramcontent.com/pod-product-compliance
Lightning Source LLC
LaVergne TN
LVHW050823061126
851857LV00012B/952